ISBN 978-1-330-26983-1
PIBN 10008007

Forgotten Books is a registered trademark of FB &c Ltd.
Copyright © 2015 FB &c Ltd.
FB &c Ltd, Dalton House, 60 Windsor Avenue, London, SW19 2RR.
Company number 08720141. Registered in England and Wales.

For support please visit www.forgottenbooks.com

1 MONTH OF
FREE
READING

at

www.ForgottenBooks.com

Similar Books Are Available from
www.forgottenbooks.com

T. JOSEPH'S ASCETICAL LIBRARY.

EDITED BY FATHERS S.J.

No. XI.

PURGATORY SURVEYED.

ROEHAMPTON :
PRINTED BY JAMES STANLEY.

PURGATORY SURVEYED:

OR,

A Particular Account of the happy, and yet thrice unhappy, state of the Souls there.

ALSO OF THE

. SINGULAR CHARITY AND WAYS WE HAVE TO RELIEVE THEM.

AND OF THE

Devotion of all ages for the Souls Departed.

WITH TWELVE EXCELLENT MEANS TO PREVENT PURGATORY, AND THE RESOLUTION OF MANY CURIOUS AND IMPORTANT POINTS.

by Etienne Binet

Edited by

W. H. ANDERDON,

Priest of the Society of Jesus.

REPRINTED FROM THE EDITION OF 1663.

LONDON:

BURNS AND OATES, PORTMAN STREET

AND PATERNOSTER ROW.

1874.

PREFACE.

THIS quaint, but forcible and edifying book, was partly translated, partly, as the translator acknowledges, "disposed, abridged, or enlarged," from a treatise by Father Stephen Binet, a French Jesuit, which is entitled " De l'estat heureux et malheureux des âmes souffrantes du Purgatoire, et des moyens souverains pour n'y aller pas, ou y demeurer fort peu ; ou sont traictées toutes les plus belles questions du Purgatoire." Paris, 1625, in 12. Douay, 1627, in 24.

Father Binet was born at Dijon in 1569, entered the Society in 1590, and, having been successively Rector of its principal houses in France, died at Paris, 1639. This treatise is numbered 20, out of 36 ascetical works composed by him, and given in De Backer's *Bibliothèque des Ecrivains de la Compagnie de Jesus.** Their titles make one wish that some competent pen may be found, to reproduce them for us in our own tongue.

* Vol. i. pp. 95—97.

The translator, who simply signs himself by the initials, R.T., was Father Richard Thimelby, also of the Society of Jesus. In those evil days, when it was death to be known to say Mass, or to reconcile any one to the true Faith, almost every priest was furnished with an *alias;* * and Father Thimelby accordingly went sometimes by the name of Ashby.† He is described in Dr. Oliver's "Collections" ‡ as being " of a genteel and ancient family in Lincolnshire." This is abundantly justified by notices occurring of

* This system of double or even treble names makes it difficult, sometimes, to ascertain the true name of a Catholic writer of that date. To take an instance or two from Oliver, occurring under the letter T, and met with in searching for the name for which R. T. might be supposed to stand : we find that John Taylor was *alias* Valentine Upsal ; that Adrian Talbot's real name was Fortescue ; that Oswald Tesimond was *alias* Greenway, *alias* Philip Beaumont ; and that John Turbeville passed under the name of Fermor.

† He was probably led to this particular name by the proximity of the village of West Ashby to that from which he derived his family name. Saunders' *History of Lincolnshire*, vol. ii. p. 98, gives us the following particulars :

"Thimbleby is about a mile north-west from Horncastle, the parishes adjoining each other. In *Domesday Book*, this place is written Stimelbi. The manor, in the reign of Charles II., was the property of Sir Robert Bolles, of Scampton," &c.

"West Ashby is a parish adjoining to the north boundaries of that of Horncastle, from which town the village is about two miles distant."

‡ "Collections towards illustrating the Biography of the Scotch, English, and Irish members of the Society of Jesus. By the Rev. Dr. Oliver. London : Dolman, 1845." The notice occurs at p. 47.

the family, at two different periods of English history. Thus :

(1.) In Sir S. Meyrick's *Heraldic Visitations of Wales, and part of the Marches,** mention is made of Richard Thumbleby (Thimbleby), knight, who was one of the bailiffs of Harddlech, or Harlech, in the county of Lincoln, and son to John Thumbleby, *armiger* to King Henry V. "It is recorded," says this writer, "I think in Camden's *Britannia*, that in the chapel of the town of Harlech (now standing, though converted into a dwelling) lies buried Sir Richard Thimbleby, who settled in that county for the purpose of enjoying the sports of hunting and hawking."

(2.) Dod's *Church History* exhibits this knightly Lincolnshire family as maintaining their hereditary spirit of loyalty, like so many other Catholic houses, during the struggles between Charles I. and his Parliament. We read there of "Charles Thimelby, a captain in the King's army, who lost his life at Worcester;" of "Robert Thimelby, a captain in the royal army, killed near Newark," and of "Nicholas Thimelby, a gentleman volunteer in the King's service, who lost his life at Bristol."†

But to return to the immediate subject of this notice. Dr. Oliver goes on to say, of Father

* Vol. ii. p. 217.
† Dod's *Church History*, vol iii. p. 67. Brussels, 1742.

Thimelby: "The Annual Letters show that he joined the Society in 1632, and describe him as *vir doctus et prudens, et amore Instituti excellens.* On 22nd November, 1646, he made the Profession of the four vows. After teaching philosophy, and discharging several collegiate offices, he was ordered to the mission, where he laboured very diligently, and chiefly in his native county. In 1666, on the death of Father William Campian, he was called over to Ghent, to be the Rector of the house of probation, and continued such until his appointment to the presidency of St. Omer's College, 28th August, 1672. There he died, 7th January, 1680, æt. 66. We have from his able pen, A Treatise on Purgatory, 8vo, London, 1663; Remarks on Stillingfleet, 4to, London, 1672."

This account seems to be taken, for the most part, from Father N. Southwell's continuation of Ribadeneira's *Bibliotheca Scriptorum Societatis Jesu;* in which we find the additional particulars, that Father Thimelby entered the Society at the age of seventeen, and taught, not only philosophy, but also polemical theology, at Louvain; and that, during his missionary life in England, he was Superior of the English Jesuits. The titles of his two works are also there given; though the former not with great accuracy. *De Felici et infelici statu animarum in Purgatorio, et [de] modo eis juvandi. Londini,* 1633, *in* 8. Item:

*Observationes generales in librum Doctoris Stillingfleti,
cum vindicatione S. Ignatii et Sociorum ejus a fœdis
maculis quibus eos ille aspergit. Londini, 1672, in 4.*

It is interesting to know that this devoted Catholic
family gave another of its sons to the priesthood, and
one, at least, of its daughters to religion. Dod gives
us the outlines of their lives :

"Edward Thimelby, of an ancient and worthy
family at Irnham, Lincolnshire. Being sent abroad
for education, he entered into an [the] ecclesiastical
state, and lived a considerable time in Rome, in the
family of an eminent Cardinal. He was afterwards
made provost of the collegiate church of St. Gery's,
in Cambray, where he died about 1690. He was a
person of remarkable piety. Some verses of his
composing may be seen in the beginning of Cressy's
Church History."

"Winifrede Thimelby, daughter of Richard
Thimelby, of Irnham, in Lincolnshire, esquire, by
Mrs. Brooksby. She became a nun in the English
monastery of St. Augustine's Order, in Louvain,
where she was chosen the third Superior. She died
August the 31st, 1690, in the seventy-second year
of her age, and fifty-five after her profession, having
been Superior twenty-two years."*

The alterations ventured upon, in this reprint,
consist chiefly in the mode of punctuation, which,

* Dod's *Church History*, vol. iii. pp. 479, 495.

being probably left to a French compositor,*
are anomalous, and often perplexing. Some expressions, so obsolete as to prevent the sense being clear,
and in the same degree lessening the value of the
book to the general reader, have been exchanged
for others in more common use. The sterling and
effective raciness of the pious author has in almost
every instance been retained. To secure timely
publication, it has been necessary to leave some
references, without sufficiently verifying them.

Let us earnestly hope that at this moment, on
the threshold of the month especially dedicated by
the Church to devotion on behalf of the holy souls,
the joint work of FF. Binet and Thimelby may
produce an abundant harvest of intercession. • If,
during their own brief time of trial, they were inspired
to put together and to enforce such powerful motives
to stir up the faithful to this devotion, will they
not now rejoice in the reproduction of their act of
zeal and charity? During the two hundred and fifty
years which have elapsed since the first publication
of the French work, many changes and revolutions
have taken place in the histories of those spots of

---

* The title-page states the book to have been printed in
Paris, in 1663 ; whereas Southwell, and Oliver after him, give
London as the place of its issue. Southwell may very naturally
have made the slip, concluding, without close observation, that
the work of an English priest would be published in London.
The date of the year is accurately given.

earth, known as France and England. But the History of Purgatory is ever the same; "happiness and unhappiness" combined; both unspeakably great; long detention, perhaps, or perhaps swift release, according to the degree of faith and charity animating the Church militant. May we now, and henceforth, realise in act, in habitual practice, and all the more from the considerations given in the following pages, the immense privilege of holding, to so great a degree, the keys of Purgatory in our hands.

W. H. A.

ROEHAMPTON,
Feast of the Most Holy Redeemer, 1874.

ADDITIONAL NOTE.

(Communicated while these sheets were passing through the press.)

THIMELBY, or Thimbleby, was the name of an ancient knightly family, seated at Pelham in Lincolnshire, in the reign of Edward III.* Towards the end of the fifteenth century, Richard Thimelby married the heiress of Sir Andrew Lutterell, knight, of Irnham in the same county. This lady brought with her, to the family into which she married, besides a claim to the barony of Lutterell, the manor of Irnham, which continued in Catholic hands until comparatively recent times. Their

* Clifford's *History of Tixall*, p. 223.

son, Richard **Thimelby**, married a daughter of Mrs. Brooksby,* daughter of Lord Vaux, of Harrowden. This Eleanor Brooksby, and her sister Anne Vaux, were Father Henry Garnet's brave and devoted benefactresses. Two of Eleanor Brooksby's grand-daughters, Winefred and Frances Thimelby, joined the English August-inianesses at Louvain; entering St. Monica's Convent in 1634 and 1642: and in 1668 Sister Winefred became Prioress of that devout and venerable house. Henry Thimelby, the younger brother of these two religious, married Gertrude, daughter of Walter, first Lord Aston of Forfar; and, on her husband's death, she entered religion in the same convent. Her niece, Catherine Aston, the daughter of her brother Herbert Aston and of Catherine Thimelby his wife, entered St. Monica's at the same time. Elizabeth, another sister, married Richard Conquest, of Houghton Conquest in Bedfordshire; and on the death, without issue, of her eldest brother's grand-daughter, Mary, the wife of Thomas Giffard of Chillington, the property passed to the Conquests. Mary Conquest, heiress of the last of that name (Benedict Conquest, who died in 1753), married Lord Arundell of Wardour; and thus Irnham passed to the Cliffords through her daughter Eleanor, wife of Lord Clifford of Ugbrooke.

Winefred, Frances, Catherine and Elizabeth Thimelby had two brothers besides Henry, already mentioned. The eldest was Sir John Thimelby, knight, with whose son John the male line of the Thimelbys expired. The other was the translator of the present work, Richard Thimelby, who entered the Society of Jesus in 1631, at the age of 17. In those times few religious men were called by their own names, and that by which Father Richard Thimelby was generally known was Ashby. He spent

* *Troubles of our Catholic Forefathers*, series 1, pp. 156, 369.

nearly fifty years in the labours of the Society, and held many important offices. He taught Philosophy at the English College at Liège, and Polemical or Controversial Theology, of which in those days there was a professorship distinct from that of Dogmatic Theology. For sixteen years he laboured on the English mission, and for some time he was Superior of the Jesuits in Lincolnshire, his native county, which was then known in the Society as "the Residence of St. Dominic." From this he passed, in 1666, to the English Novitiate at Watten in Flanders, where he was Rector and Master of Novices for six years. On the 28th of August, 1672, he was transferred to the English College at St. Omer's, the Rectorship of which he held for another period of six years. He was relieved of this charge some months before his death, which took place at St. Omer's on the 7th of January, 1679-80. This good Father was professed of the four vows, November 22, 1646. The records of the Society speak in the highest terms of praise of his learning, prudence, and religious spirit; but the list of the offices he held, speak more eloquently than words of the esteem in which he was held as a spiritual man.

Several other Catholics of the name are mentioned, but their connection with this branch of the family is not clear. Edward Thimbelby, who died in 1690, Provost of St. Gery or Gaugericus in Cambray, may have been another brother. Three officers of the Royal army, Charles, Robert and Nicholas Thimelby, lost their lives in the Civil War. There was one Gabriel Thimelby, who died a still more glorious death, and may be called a martyr, as he is recorded to have died in prison in the year 1586. Unfortunately, all that we know of him is, that he was once a student in the College at Rheims.

A PREFATORY ADDRESS TO THE CATHOLIC READER.

———

DEAR READER,

The drift of this treatise is not to prove Purgatory: but, taking it for granted, as a prime maxim of Catholicism, that God has a suffering Church in the other world, besides that which triumphs in heaven, and that which is militant here upon earth, the design is to set it forth in such lively colours, as may not only express its nature (as far as we are able to judge of it, at so great a distance) but raise your thoughts, first to a compassionate care for the present, of procuring all possible relief for such distressed souls as are already fallen under the lash of those merciless torments, and secondly, to a provident prevention for the future, that the like mischief may not involve yourselves hereafter. Now, this being the chief aim of these my labours, I am put upon a kind of necessity of giving you the trouble of this prefatory address. For, should this Survey of Purgatory fall into any other hands but yours, it could look for no better entertainment than to be laid aside for waste paper, such as would befall some strange map or survey of another world, which had no other existence but in the brains of the painter. For why should the enemies of truth, whose belief reaches only to heaven and hell, amuse themselves with the consideration of a third place, for which they can find no place in their creed? And yet, though I presume that this will be its common fate, when it meets with such persons, yet I am very confident the judicious Protestant, if he can but find in his heart to peruse these papers, especially the Fifth Survey, will find more than enough to convince him of this middle state of souls, which we call Purgatory.

Now, to say the truth of this treatise, I know not well how to profess myself the author, nor yet the translator, of it. Not author; for I must acknowledge the main bulk and substance of what I offer to be borrowed of the Revered Father Stephen Binet, of the Society of Jesus. Not a bare translator; because I am to do myself so much right as to tell you, that I have not tied myself so wholly to that worthy person's method or matter, as not to yield a little now and then to my own genius; but have so made use of his learned pen, as to dispose, abridge or enlarge, where I took it to be more for your satisfaction, in this conjuncture of time and place wherein I was to publish it.

As for the language, I have taken care neither to have it so bald as not to suit a little with this eloquent age we live in, nor yet so flourishing and luxuriant as to dry up the fountains of devotion, which I seek to open. And if all my endeavours prove but so happy as to occasion the releasing of any one soul out of Purgatory, or the conveying of any other into heaven without passing that way, I have my end, which is only the greater glory of God, and the good of souls. There was a Roman Emperor who would never dine but he would be feeding his thoughts with the contemplation of the torments of hell, and the pleasures of the Elysian fields, which he had caused to be curiously painted and exposed for that purpose in his dining-room. I do not press you to use

any such devotions or pictures; I only offer you this
Survey of Purgatory; which I beseech you to look upon;
and withal to have an eye still upon heaven, and the best
means how to send souls thither, and to follow them yourselves, without stepping aside into Purgatory; for, believe
it, if you come once there, you will find it a very restless
and uncomfortable lodging, which I pray God you may
all timely prevent; and I earnestly beg your good prayers
that the like mercy may not be denied to

Your most devoted servant,

R. T.

CONTENTS.

THE THIRD SURVEY.

THE FOURTH SURVEY.

THE CONCLUSION.

PURGATORY . SURVEYED

THE FIRST SURVEY.

PURGATORY IS LAID OPEN, WITH ALL THE HELLISH PAINS WITH WHICH THE SOULS ARE TORMENTED.

FOR fear lest my discourses, dear reader, should not prove so lucky as to raise up your compassion, nor my words so prevalent as to make a breach or deep impression in thy heart, which is the main thing I aim at in this whole treatise, I am resolved to have recourse to that pious stratagem which the first Jesuits so happily made use of in the conversion of the Indies. Those good fathers were not, at first, well skilled in the language of the New World; and yet their zeal would be still carrying them on to preach, whilst the Indians stood listening and staring at them, but could understand little or nothing. This would not have done their work, had they not withal used this device, to take with them into the pulpit certain devout pictures which they had carried out of Europe, in which the Passion of our Blessed Saviour was very lively represented. Here they first showed the most bitter torments which the Son of God endured for

B

their sakes; and then they laboured to express, in their best Indian phrase, the name of God, Saviour of the world, most holy Prophet, and the like; pointing still at the picture, to tell them that He whom they saw so cruelly misused was the very Man they spake of. And this they followed with showers of tears; preaching Christ's Passion more with their eyes than their tongues, and setting forth their discourses with sighs and sobs and a mournful voice, in lieu of other tropes and metaphors. Who would believe it? The barbarians, at the sight of so lamentable a spectacle, out of a natural compassion, seconded by an interior impulse of divine Grace, burst forth into fountains of tears, and became strangely concerned for that poor Patient, whom they beheld only in effigy. The heart has this property, that it understands the language of hearts, let the expressions of the tongue be never so imperfect; and the eyes are of that sympathetic nature, that when eyes speak to them in floods of tears, in lieu of full periods, they instantly melt also into tears, and so mingle their griefs with a strange kind of sympathy and near alliance. What the tongue cannot utter, the eye speaks aloud; and the heart, and the very air of the whole countenance, of a man who seems to carry his very heart on his brow. Seeing, therefore, my discourses may fall short of what I design, I am now going about to lay Purgatory open: to represent, I say, unto your view, as in a map or picture, that bloody tragedy which is acted there, not in sport and merriment, alas! but with horror and amazement. And if you dare not with the eye of faith contemplate this sad and horrid spectacle in itself, at least refuse not to look upon this picture, which I am going to delineate, to give you a rude draught of the just rigour of Almighty God in purging holy souls, and, as it were, distilling them by drops in a fiery limbeck.

§ 1.—*Of the fire of Purgatory, and pain of sense.*

It was a strage piece of niceness,* that of the Grecians in the Council of Florence, to boggle at the smoke and fire of Purgatory, and yet withal to confess it to be a dark and dreadful dungeon, an abyss of utter grief and torments ; as if they would have been content all other engines of cruelty should have place there, to play the executioners, so they might but have leave to banish fire from having anything to do in the purgation of souls. The Latin Fathers laboured to undeceive them in this point of folly, and sore gravelled them with that text of the Apostle · " He shall be saved, yet so as by fire :"† which cannot be meant of hell-fire, as the Grecians understood it, because no salvation or redemption is to be expected there ; but may well be meant of the fire of Purgatory, which is designed only for the purifying of saved souls. And though they thought fit afterwards to waive that controversy for peace' sake, and not to press on to a definition, yet is it a doctrine very generally received and taught· by the holy Fathers and Doctors of the Catholic Church, and very consonant to the dictates of the Holy Ghost

---

* *i.e.* An over-subtle and inconsistent distinction.
† I Cor. iii. 15.

in Divine Scriptures, that there is a real and corporeal
fire in Purgatory ; and that the souls which depart this
life, without first cancelling their many failings and
imperfections by satisfactory works, are necessarily
plunged into merciless flames, which, by little and
little, eat away all that dross and impurity which, till
expiated, obstructs their entrance into heaven.   Nor
is it possible, to my thinking, to raise any argument
of substance* to discredit these purging flames, which
will not also be levelled at the extinguishing of hell-
fire : which, notwithstanding, Holy Writ assures us to
be " prepared for the devil and his angels."† I am
sure St. Augustine‡ finds the same difficulty, how the
devils' and men's souls can be tormented with fire ;
and gives the same solution to both, with a " Why
should we not say that incorporeal spirits may be
truly tormented with corporeal fire, though after a
strange and wonderful manner ?"   Must we presently
renounce the Oracles of God's Church, because we
cannot fathom them with our narrow capacity ?   The
very foundations of our Faith would be shrewdly§
shaken, should we measure them by this preposterous
rule, of a seeming demonstration to the contrary.
Believe it, it is one of the first rudiments, but main
principles, of a Christian, to captivate his understanding, and so regulate all his dictamens, that they be

* *i.e.* Any valid argument.
† St. Matt. xxv. 41.
‡ *De Civit.* xxi. 10.   "*Veris, sed miris modis.*"
§ The word is applied in old English as meaning *greatly* or
forcibly, but in an unfavourable sense, implying pain, grievous-
ness, contention, &c.

sure to run parallel with the sentiments of the Church. And this I take to be the case when the question is started about Purgatory fire, which I shall ever reckon in the class of those truths which cannot be contradicted without manifest temerity; as being the doctrine generally preached and taught all over Christendom.

You must, then, conceive Purgatory to be a vast, darksome and hideous chaos, full of fire and flames, in which the souls are kept close prisoners until they have fully satisfied for all their misdemeanours, according to the estimate of Divine justice. For God has made choice of this element of fire wherewith to punish souls, because it is the most active, piercing, sensible,* and insupportable of all others. But that which quickens it indeed, and gives it more life, is this: that it acts as the instrument of God's justice, who, by His omnipotent power, heightens and reinforces its activity as He pleases, and so makes it capable to act upon bodiless spirits. Do not then look only upon this fire, though in good earnest it be dreadful enough of itself; but consider the Arm that is stretched out, and the Hand that strikes, and the rigour of God's infinite justice, who, through this element of fire, vents His wrath, and pours out whole tempests of His most severe and yet most just vengeance. So that the fire works as much mischief,† as I may say, to the souls, as God commands; and He commands as much as is due; and as much is due as the sentence bears: a sentence irrevocably

* *i.e.* Apprehended by the senses.
† *i.e.* Not implying injury, far less injustice; but simply punishment and suffering.

pronounced at the high tribunal of the severe and
rigorous justice of an angry God, and whose anger
is so prevalent, that the Holy Scripture styles it "a
day of fury."* Now you will easily believe that this
fire is a most horrible punishment in its own nature;
but you may do well to reflect also on that which
I have now suggested, that the fury of Almighty
God is, as it were, the fire of this fire, and the heat
of its heat; and that He serves Himself of it as He
pleases, by doubling and redoubling its sharp pointed
forces; for this is that which makes it the more
grievous and insupportable to the souls that are thus
miserably confined and imprisoned.

They were not much out of the way, that styled
Purgatory a transitory kind of hell, because the
principal pains of the damned are to be found there;
with this only difference, that in hell they are eternal
and in Purgatory they are only transitory and fleeting:
for otherwise † it is probably the very same fire which
burns both the holy souls and the damned spirits; ‡
and the pain of loss is, in both places, the chief
torment, as I shall declare hereafter. Now, does
not your hair stand on end? does not your heart
tremble, when you hear that the poor souls in Purgatory are tormented with the same or the like flames
to those of the damned? Can you refrain from crying
out, with the Prophet Isaias: "Who can dwell with
such devouring fire, and unquenchable burnings?"§

* Job xx. 28; Isaias xiii. 13; Lam. i. 12.
† *i.e.* As to the other particulars.
‡ Suarez, d. 45, sec. 2, n. 4; St. Thomas in 4, d. 21, q. 1.
§ Isaias xxxiii. 14.

Heavens! what a lamentable case is this! Those miserable souls, who of late, when they were wedded to their bodies, were so nice and dainty, forsooth, that they durst scarce venture to enjoy the comfortable heat of a fire, but under the protection of their screens and their fans, for fear of sullying their complexions, and if by chance a spark had been so rude as to light upon them, or a little smoke, it was not to be endured: those, for whom down itself was too hard, and even ready to break their bones, one single grain of misfortune, a stone but as big as a nut, a rotten tooth, a sullen and malignant humour stolen into the marrow of a bone, a cross word, an affront, an idle fancy, a mere dream, was enough to bury their whole felicity in a kind of hell:—alas! how will it fare with them, when they shall see themselves tied to unmerciful firebrands, or imbodied, as it were, with flames of fire, surrounded with frightful darkness, broiled and consumed without intermission, and perhaps condemned to the same fire with which the devils are unspeakably tormented? When Saul found himself beset on all sides, and in the midst of his enemies, and saw that he must either die instantly, or fall into the hands of that base and accursed crew · Oh, let me rather die, cried he;* he will do me a favour that will cut my throat, that so I may not see myself butchered by such wicked hands, and trailed away by them; death is not the thing I apprehend, but that, a king as I am, I should die like a slave! ah, it is that which gives me the fatal blow, and breaks my very heart. O God! what a confusion, what a sensible

* 1 Kings xxxi. 4.

heart-breaking will it be to these noble and generous souls, designed to eternal glory in the kingdom of heaven, when they shall see themselves condemned to the same punishment, and devoured by the same implacable flames, with those of the damned, and lodged in the very suburbs of hell. A prince had rather die a thousand deaths than be condemned to live amongst base slaves in a galley, or be hanged amongst felons: for it is not the death so much as the dishonour that makes them to die indeed. And can you doubt whether the souls of the just have the same feelings, when they see themselves involved in the same misfortune, in the same place, and in the same flames of fire, with which the accursed rabble of damned spirits is eternally tormented? Ah! they take it for so high a dishonour, that it may with reason be questioned whether this unhappy place and condition grieves them not more than the fire itself Once* on a time, they would have forced a young Roman cavalier into the bottom of a dark and stinking pit; but his heart was so filled with indignation at it, that he chose rather to dash out his brains against a door-threshold, and so to let out his blood and his life together, than to enter into so noisome a place. What a tearing grief must it be to those virtuous souls, when they shall see themselves border upon the very confines of hell, and in that accursed frontier: and, more than this, to be shut up close prisoners in that unhappy gulf; and to be condemned to suffer the same fire as the damned, though their punishment be neither so terrible nor so lasting!

* Plutarch, *Sen.*

Good God! how the great Saints and Doctors astonish me, when they treat .of this fire, and of the pain of sense, as they call it. For they peremptorilv pronounce, that the fire that purges those souls, those both happy and unhappy souls, surpasses all the torments which are to be found in this miserable life of man, or are possible to be invented; for so far they go. Out of which assertion it clearly follows, that the furious fits of the stone, fever, or raging gout, the tormenting colic, with all the horrible convulsions. of the worst of diseases, nay, though you join racks,, gridirons, boiling oils, wild beasts, and a hundred horses drawing several ways and tearing one limb from another, with all the other hellish devices of the most barbarous and cruel tyrants, all this does not reach to the least part of the mildest pains in Purgatory. For thus they discourse : the fire and the pains of the other world, are of another nature from those of this life ; because God elevates them above their nature to be instruments of His severity. Now, say they, things of an inferior degree can never reach to the power of such things as are of a higher rank ; for example, the air, let it be ever so inflamed, unless it be converted into fire, can never be so hot as fire. Besides, God bridles His rigour in this world; but, in the next, He lets the reins loose, and punishes almost equally to the desert. And, since those souls have preferred creatures before their Creator, He seems to be put upon a necessity of punishing them beyond the ordinary strength of creatures : and hence it is, that the fire of Purgatory burns more, torments and afflicts more, then all the creatures of this life are

able to do.   But is it really true, that the least pain
in Purgatory exceeds the greatest here upon earth?
O God! the very statement makes me tremble for fear,
and my very heart freezes into ice with astonishment.
And yet, who dare oppose St. Augustine, St. Thomas,
St. Anselm, St. Gregory the Great?*   Is there any
hope of carrying the negative assertion against such
a stream of Doctors, who all maintain the affirmative,
and bring so strong reasons for it?   Have patience to
hear them once more.   Sin, say they, exceeds all
creatures in malice ; and therefore, let it be never so
little, it must deserve a punishment exceeding all the
pain that can proceed from creatures.   Again :
Creatures, here below, do nothing above their natural
reach and capacity; they act only within the sphere of
their limited forces : whereas, the fire that is designed
to purify guilty souls, derives its vigour and force
from God ; who, being Almighty, and, besides, pro-
voked to displeasure, makes it so active and so
forcible, that there is nothing that can be compared
with it.   And they add unto all this a world of
visions and revelations, which seem to countenance
the rigour of their statement.   What then will become
of thee, poor idle soul, if the least pains in Purgatory
surpass the greatest in this world? what, I say, will
become of thee, that art so tender, that a little smoke
is able to draw tears from thy eyes ?

    But, for thy comfort, there are Doctors in the
Catholic Church that cannot agree with so much

----

* S. Augustine in Psalm xxxvii. ; St. Thomas, *Suppl.* q. 100,
a. 3, et in 4, d. 21 ;   St. Gregory in Psalm iii. *Penitent.;*
St. Anselm in *Elucidario.*

severity: and, namely, St. Bonaventure, who is very
peremptory in denying it.* For what way is there,
says this holy Doctor, to verify so great a paradox,
without wounding reason, and destroying the infinite
mercy of God? I am easily persuaded there are
torments in Purgatory far exceeding any in this mortal
life; this is most certain, and it is but reasonable it
should be so: but that the least there should be more
terrible than the most terrible in the world, cannot
enter into my belief. May it not often fall out, that
a man comes to die in a most eminent state of
perfection; save only, that in his last agony, out of
mere frailty, he commits a venial sin, or carries along
with him some relic of his former failings, which
might have been easily blotted out with a *Pater
noster*, or washed away with a little holy water: for
I am supposing it to be some very small matter. Now
what likelihood is there, I will not say, that the infinite
mercy of God, but that the very rigour of His justice,
though you conceive it to be ever so severe, should
inflict so horrible a punishment upon this holy soul,
as not to be equalled by the greatest torments in this
life; and all this for some petty fault, scarce worth the
speaking of? How! would you have God, for a kind
of trifle, to punish a soul full of grace and virtue, and
so severely to punish her, as to exceed all the racks,
caldrons, furnaces, and other hellish inventions, which
are scarce inflicted upon the most execrable criminals
in the world? What do you make God to be? Is
He not a God of mercy in the other world as well
as in this? He that is so sweet and so good, says

* St. Bonaventure in 4, d. 20.

Tertullian,* that He darts the rays of His mercies into the darkest abyss of hell, shall He be so extremely rigorous in Purgatory, which is so full of Saints? That which a sigh would have blown away here, or a tear have drowned, as being so small a matter, will you have God pour out His whole wrath for it, and to punish it with such a proportion of sufferings, as cannot be paralleled by all the torments in this world? Have a care lest, by making God too severe, you say that which clashes with His infinite mercy. That nothing should remain unpunished, is no more than fitting : but that for a mere peccadillo, or for some small remnant of a little penance, God should employ such tortures, is a most incredible paradox, and St. Bonaventure will not believe it : and are we not beholden to him for it? He confesses that the fire, the worm, and all the purging pain, is of its nature far greater than the pains of this world ; but that the least there should surpass the greatest here, he flatly denies ; and I cannot think thou wilt need much entreaty to side with him. And thus much learned Suarez† has prudently observed for thy purpose ; that in truth, the pains of Purgatory and those of this life are of quite different kinds, and can no more be compared together than a flint with a diamond; but that there may be so many flints put together as to exceed the worth of a diamond : and so may the pains of this life be so multiplied, as to surmount the least of those in Purgatory.

* Tertullian, *Apol.*   † Suarez, d. 40, 3, 4.

§ 2.—*Of the worm, and pain of loss.*

But why do I entertain you so long with the consideration of the fire and flames of Purgatory, as if it were the only or the greatest torment of the afflicted souls? Alas, there is a worm which gnaws them yet more to the quick than those murdering flames, which make but an outward assault. It is this worm, alas, it is this worm that plays the tyrant over those captive souls. The worm of hell shall never die:* while that of Purgatory shall die, indeed, but so long as it lives it is not to be imagined how cruelly it bites. I know there are those among the learned that believe God has in store certain ravenous and devouring worms, that shall incessantly prey upon the carcases of the damned souls, and cause an endless martyrdom by consuming them without ever yet consuming them. But as for Purgatory, where there are only mere souls, stripped of their bodies, there are no corporeal worms; but the worm that gnaws them is a metaphorical worm, or a sharp and sensible grief and deep resentment,† which utterly undoes those miserable souls by piercing and transpiercing them with the sharp lances of a thousand and a thousand remorses.

But to give you, in fine, a more particular description of this insatiable and devouring worm, which causes them so much mischief and vexation: divines teach us that it is either an heroical act of charity; or

* Isaias lxvi. 24; St. Mark ix. 45.
† *i.e.* A continued feeling of pain for something that has taken place.

a vigorous act of contrition; or, finally, a holy kind of
impatience and supernatural act of hope; but such a
one as does so importunely and powerfully chastise
them, that it is not to be expressed. You may fancy
charity to be a golden file, which goes filing and still
filing away the dross of their imperfections, and as it
were consuming them without intermission; contrition
to be a pair of hot, biting pincers, which doth so desperately pinch those poor souls that it is a kind of
pity to God and His angels to behold it; hope
retarded to be a kind of rack, upon which those
miserable souls are so far extended and stretched out
with a desire that carries them to God, and so with-
held by the impediment that lies in themselves, that it
must needs be an unmerciful torment. They seem,
as it were, to be drawn in pieces by wild horses.
Love draws, but pain withdraws; contrition spurs
them on, but their misfortune pulls them back; hope
gives them wings, but justice clips them off; and,
through the violence of these contrary motions, these
unfortunate souls are in a most lamentable condition,
and, as the Holy Scripture expresses it, are gnawn
and torn in pieces with hungry, devouring, and tormenting worms. It is not the fire, nor all the brimstone and tortures they endure, which murders them
alive. No, no ; it is the domestical cause of all these
mischiefs that racks their consciences and is their
cruelest executioner. This, this is the greatest of
their evils; for a soul that has shaken off the fetters
of flesh and blood, and is full of the love of God, no
more disordered with unruly passions, nor blinded
with the night of ignorance, sees clearly the vast injury

she has done herself to have offended so good a God, and to have deserved to be thus banished out of His sight and deprived of that divine fruition. She sees how easily she might have flown up straight to heaven at her first parting with her body, and what a trifle it was that impeded her. A moment lost, of those inebriating joys, seems to her now worthy to be redeemed with an eternity of pains. Then, reflecting with herself that she was created only for God, and cannot be truly satisfied but by enjoying God, and that out of Him all this goodly machine of the world is no better than a direct hell, and an abyss of evils : alas! what worms, what martyrdoms, and what nipping pincers, are such pinching thoughts as these? The fire is to her but as smoke, in comparison of this vexing remembrance of her own follies, which betrayed her to this disgraceful and unavoidable misfortune. There was a king who in a humour* gave away his crown and his whole estate for the present refreshment of a cup of cold water ; but, returning a little to himself, and soberly reflecting what he had done, had like to have run stark mad, to see the strange, irreparable folly he had committed. To lose a year, or two years (to say no more), the beatifical vision, for a glass of water, for a handful of earth, for the love of a fading beauty, for a little air of worldly praise, a mere puff of honour ; ah! it is the hell of Purgatory to a soul that truly loves God, and frames a right conceit of things. Jephte† could have died for grief, when he saw that by his rashness he was to lose his only daughter, the light of his eyes, the life of his soul, and soul of his.

* *i.e.* In a momentary fancy.   † Judges xi. and xviii.

life. And that poor youth from whom they had stolen
his gods, although they were mere idols, yet did he
take on most bitterly, and became so disconsolate,
there was no chiding him out of that humour. "What!"
said he, "have you robbed me of my gods, and do
you now question me, why I lament?" As if he had
not cause enough to grieve, who has lost his gods.
And you may observe, it was not his fault that they
were lost; and besides, they were but gods of wood
and stone, such as a skilful artist would have made
far better. The case here is different; for the souls
clearly see they have lost God through their own carelessness; and lost Him for ten, twenty, or perhaps
thirty years, and this puts them out of the reach of all
comfort. Here below, indeed, we are not able to
taste the bitterness of this wormwood; but those pure
souls, who are in the grace of God, and full of light,
and well grounded discourses, see so clearly the gross-
ness and foulness of this error, and taste so sensibly
the gall and bitterness thereof, that it is a more vexing
pain to them than that of the fire.

But you will say: It is but for a short time that
they are to be kept out of Paradise. O God! this is
enough to break their hearts; for, in that short time
you speak of, they could have exercised a million of
most refined, heroical, and divine acts in heaven: and
all this is lost. And if one act of virtue here on earth
gives so much glory to God and so much joy to the
whole Court of heaven, what a loss is it, to have care-
lessly let slip the occasion of exercising a million of
such acts in heaven, which can never be recalled! I
speak not for the merit, nor for the content there is in

doing well, nor for the degrees of glory which are lost.
No, I touch not yet what concerns their interest; but
I only treat of the glory which they might have given
to God by their signal services of love and adoration;
all which precious treasure is negligently cast away.
When that good poor widow cast her two brass mites
into the treasury,* Christ Jesus was as well pleased as
if she had cast in both her eyes, or as many worlds.
And when St. Martin cut his cloak in two, to give one
half of it to a needy beggar, our Blessed Saviour vouchsafed to clothe Himself with that half garment, and
turning to the Angels, who were about Him in great
numbers, and withal showing them that livery of His
servant; "Behold," said He, "how nobly this young
catechumen has attired Me." If the Almighty
Monarch of the world makes so great a reckoning
of one act of virtue, one small charity, what vexation
will it breed in a soul of the other world, to consider
that other glorious souls, and perhaps some of her
alliance or acquaintance, are already daily spending
themselves in acts of highest perfection, and that she
has wilfully thrown away all this glory, which she
might have given to Almighty God; and in place of
acting so gloriously in the empyrean heaven, all re-
splendent with divine fire, she is constrained to lie
parching and frying in the flames of Purgatory, and
undergoing a thousand inconsolable punishments.

Now, if you lay on the back of this the consideration
of interest; good God! what a terrible grief will it be
to holy souls, to reflect on the loss of so many degrees
of grace and glory, which they have foolishly and

* St. Mark xii. 42; St. Luke xxi. 2.

negligently cast away, for mere trifles, and without
hope of recovery! One grain of grace is certainly
more worth than all the world. What a misery, then,
what a grief, and what a confusion will it be, to have
prodigally sold, for nothing, so many grains, so many
graces, and so many worlds of true happiness? "Since
I have lost my empire," cried Nero, "there is no
living for me." "Could I but one day arrive to be
King of Athens," said a Grecian, "I could be content
to walk barefoot to the bottomless pit of hell: so great
a value do I set upon swaying the sceptre but one
day; and so precious is the least grain of glory in my
estimation." Now, if these ambitious souls have such
feelings for a little vain and transitory glory, what will
they have, who breath nothing but the pure love of
God, and know how to set a true value upon glory,
in those heavenly mansions? This, in the opinion of
learned Suarez, is a worm, the most sensible,* and the
most vexatious of all others, in that Church of patient
sufferers.

But since these two worms, Love and Grief, combine together, to martyr those poor souls, which of
the two is the most grievous; charity, or contrition?
They have neither of them teeth to bite with; but they
conjure up such tempests of biting thoughts, in these
unfortunate souls, as give them a world of afflictions.
Methinks I hear them discourse, in their turns, much
after this fashion ·

Love. O ungrateful and disloyal soul! hast thou
so easily lost the sight of thy merciful Redeemer?

Grief. Die for shame, unlucky soul! and die for

* As above, p. 5.

grief, for having so easily merited that God should thus banish thee in these base flames.

Love. What hast thou got, by losing so good a God, whom thou wert already to have possessed and enjoyed?

Grief. What hast thou got, but deadly heart-breakings, for having preferred sin before His infinite favours?

Love. In lieu of riding upon the wings of Seraphim, and burning with love, as they do in heaven, miserable creature! thou art now to be locked up under ground, in a furnace of hellish flames.

Grief. In lieu of calling to mind the benefits of this great God, thou art to be gnawn to the very heart, with the sharp teeth of an infamous grief, and to pass so many whole days in sighs and sobs, and unprofitable lamentations.

Love. So many lesser souls have taken their flight straight up into heaven; and what! dost thou stick there below, in those loathsome pits of fire?

Grief. So many simple idiots, by leading innocent lives, are now in glory; whilst thou, idle wretch, liest there melting in unquenchable flames.

Love. What a madness was it for thee, to cast away so many precious hours of seeing God; when one glimpse of that Divine Object is worth a million of worlds?

Grief. Could there be a greater folly, than, for a slight pastime, to offend so loving a Father, and put Him upon a necessity of punishing thee here like a criminal, to wear off thy felonious and rebellious offences?

Love. What is become of so many degrees of glory,

C 2

so many ecstatical acts, so many divine canticles, which thou shouldst have sung in heaven, since thou art buried underground, in a sulphureous lake?

Grief. What is become of all thy cursed possessions, which now persecute thy soul with a fresh remembrance of thy sottish disloyalty?

Love. Thou wert created for God; canst thou live without Him, and without glassing thyself in that eternal mirror, and sparkling rays of His divine countenance?

Grief. Thou wert placed in the sublunary world to serve Him; canst thou, without swooning for grief, call to mind the life which thou hast led; and is not the remembrance of thy excesses more frightful to thee than the very sight of hell itself?

Love. He that loves God, had rather sink down into a thousand hells, than lose Him for a moment.

Grief. He that loves God, had rather eternally suffer all the torments of hell, than lie one instant in the hell of hells; that is, in the bosom of a mortal sin.

Thus violently do these two virtues, of Love and Grief, make their several onsets on this poor soul; thus terribly do they bait her, one after another; thus cruelly do they lay her under the heavy press of unavoidable reproaches.

This is not all: for divines teach, and are peremptory upon the matter, that the more a soul loves God, and the greater Saint she is, the more sensible is she of the biting of these unmerciful worms. And, by the way, you are to note that these holy souls do not suffer these afflictions only to purge themselves. No; though there were no other motive but that of the love of God, and a certain honesty* well becoming their noble nature; though there were nothing to be got by it; yet would they not desist from exercising these generous and heroical acts, and from giving God a signal testimony of the dear affection of their souls. In the meantime, this their honesty costs them dear; and these acts of charity and contrition are extreme painful. And since the sting of honour wounds deeper, pains sorer, and goes more to the quick, than 'pain itself, hence it follows that these holy souls, whether for love or for justice' sake, are upon a most cruel rack, and so become an object of great commiseration; and it cannot be expressed how beholden they reckon themselves to those that endeavour to comfort them, and are mindful of their calamity. Now, the reason why divines believe that the most perfect souls are the most afflicted with these voluntary kinds of punishments, as I may term them, is, because they all actuate† according to the uttermost sphere and extent of their virtue; so that a soul that has a greater proportion of love, acts with more vigour, and plunges herself deeper in the profound abyss of love, and in the gall and bitterness of contrition. And, as this proceeds out of mere love, notwithstanding their so sensible misfortune, they would not lose an ounce of it: so tender is their love to God, and so great the horror they have of all that is displeasing in His sight. But of this more at large hereafter

Now I must tell you plainly, all that I have yet said is, in a manner, nothing to what I am going to say.

* *i.e.* Sense of what is worthy and befitting.
† *i.e.* Produce their acts.

The Saints and Doctors of God's Church, as I have
already insinuated, unanimously agree, that the most
grievous pain in Purgatory is to be deprived, for a
time, of the beatifical vision, and to be laid aside, and
banished, as unworthy to contemplate the bright.Sun
of the Divinity.   This pain of loss, as they call it, is
the pain of pains ; it is the deepest pit of Purgatory,
and the very bellows that blow the coals there.   This
evil, of the privation of the sight of God, is, according
to St. Thomas,* of its own nature far exceeding all
the temporal punishments of this world : and thus he
proves it.   Will you know the full latitude of grief,
and take an exact survey of all its dimensions?
Reflect with yourself, what is the good which it
deprives us of, what the present evil we endure, what
powerful instinct we have to repossess that good
which we have lost, what obligation we have•there-
unto both by grace and nature ; and lastly, what a
violent application and vigour of spirit we feel in
our souls, in the pursuit of it.   Now all this is
extreme, in the evil we now treat of.   For it is the
precious sight of God which is lost, who is the con-
summation of all bliss ; it is the very dregs of bitterness those poor souls drink down at large draughts ;
it is the only beautiful Object, for which they were
created, and redeemed with the most precious Blood
of Christ, for which they breathed out so many sighs
in this mortal life, and which they do so passionately
pursue, when once delivered out of their bodies, that
there is nothing to be compared to that holy ardour.
No ; I do not think that an arrow shot from a bow,

* St. Thomas in 4, a. 21, a. 1.

or an eagle upon the wing, or the wind, or lightning, or the sun in his full career or flight itself, flies away faster. I cannot believe that fire mounts up, or a stone sinks down to its centre, with more vehemency, nor that the heavens can be swifter in their motions, then these vigorous souls are in running, flying, and precipitating themselves into God—when, alas! they find their wings' clipped, and their whole flight so unhappily stopped, that no tongue is able to express the resentment* they feel at it.

I know that St. Bonaventure strives to sweeten this martyrdom; and will not have this privation, or pain of loss, to be so cruel as others make it: and in particular he maintains that it does not always exceed the greatest torments of this life. I will not take upon me the boldness, to make myself judge and umpire between St. Thomas and St. Bonaventure; that is to say, between an angel and a seraph, an angelical doctor and a seraphical doctor; in a word, between two famous oracles of divinity, two glorious suns placed in the several spheres of their religious Orders. But what remedy? whether of the two shall we believe? The one assures us, that the privation of the sight of God is a martyrdom beyond all the martyrdoms of this world; the other tells us for a truth that it were certainly a most grievous torment, but that it is sometimes so tempered and alleviated by other considerations, that it equals not the severest rigour of the torments of this world. What? is there no means to reconcile these two heavenly Doctors? May we not say, they have both reason

* As above, p. 13.

on their sides? They have both won, and both lost
the field ; and, whilst the one looks as it were to the
north, and the other to the south, they both meet in
the meridian line of charity, and rest securely in the
bosom of the same truth. St. Thomas means to say,
that if you look upon this privation, as it relates to
God, the loss is incomparable; and he speaks the
very truth : that the soul has not a more violent
instinct, than that which carries her to God, this is
also an undoubted truth ; that there cannot be a
heavier loss than that of God; and is not this also
clear? that, unless this grief be otherwise moderated,
it is the most intolerable of all others ; this is as
evident as the rest : that you cannot deprive a soul
of a more lovely object, and consequently, that there
is not the thing in this world whose absence is of
its nature so sensible ;* who can doubt of all this?
Certainly, if you state the case thus, and go no
further, St. Thomas has clearly got the victory. Now
let us hear St. Bonaventure, who tells us that this
evil of privation, being joined with a most certain
hope of seeing God ere long, may be much lessened ;
that, even in this world, we lack the sight of God,
and yet by reason of other diversions,† are not so
much concerned for it; that the holy souls most
contentedly submit themselves to this piece of
severity, and the more willingly they do it, the less
are they burdened with sorrow ; that many Saints, out
of pure charity, and for the glory of God, have offered
themselves to be thus eternally deprived of the sight
of God, and have taken great pleasure in it; with a

* *i.e.* So deeply to be felt.　† *i.e.* Objects distracting the attention.

world of other reasons, of which I shall treat in the next Survey, where I muster up the comforts of the souls in Purgatory. Has he not reason for all this, I pray you? Nay, have they not both reason for what they teach? Methinks, they do like those that look upon your pictures, which are drawn after the Italian fashion, by mathematical projection; one looks upon them this way, and sees a fair picture of St. Michael; another that way, and sees St. Laurence upon a gridiron, represented to the life. The one vows he sees an angel, and he says true; the other is ready to swear he sees a martyr, and he is not mistaken: meanwhile, they contest about it, and neither of them will forsake his opinion, whilst both are in the right, though they seem to wrong one another. Let us therefore conclude, that in truth there is something in this pain of loss, which surpasses all that can be imagined in this world; but that God is pleased in some cases to mingle certain comfortable sweets with it, which take off much of the bitterness which the souls would otherwise find therein.

§ 3.—*Other considerations, much aggravating these pains.*

But that which adds new life and strength to these quick and piercing pains is, to see that they have not only wilfully lost for ever so many degrees of glory, whereof the least is an inestimable treasure, but are also estranged from the sight of God, by their own carelessness and tepidity. To forego the sight of God, out of charity, is to find a kind of paradise in hell; but

to lose the sight of God by one's own fault, though it
be but for a moment, is a hell indeed to a soul that
loves.   Naturalists tell us of a little bird that is so far
in love with the sun, that she lives no longer than she
can behold it, and so lives but a few hours ; for no
sooner does the sun set, but the poor bird, seeing no
longer the living rays of the sun, believing it to be
really dead, dies also, as not being able to survive
the sole object of its love.   God is the Sun of our
souls : and therefore these worthy souls, seeing this
Sun quite eclipsed from their eyes, and overcast with
the sable night of a suffering people, would doubtless
die if they could.   For, God being the life of their
life, having lost this life, how should they live ?   When
the Blessed Virgin and St. Joseph had lost sight of
the little Infant Jesus, what tongue can express the
affliction of their souls ?   He only knows, who has
tried it by experience, and whose eyes God has
opened, what it is to lose the sight of God, and to
lose it through his own fault, and to be, as it were,
pointed at for a wretch that has lost his God.

I wept, says holy David,* and I wept night and
day, when they would be still thus upbraiding me :
Why, David, where is thy God ? the God for whom
thou hadst so much love ?   Oh, it is a dagger at my
very heart, and they kill me when they ask me the
question.   Now, this dagger is never out of the hearts
of those desolate and languishing souls.   "I will either
die this day," cried Cæsar, " or I will be the chief in
Rome ; for what likelihood is there that Cæsar should
live, and not be Cæsar ; live, and not live in the

* Psalm xli. 4.

quality which is due to his birth and courage?" Oh, how often does this thought assault and persecute these holy souls · "Alas! how easily could I have purchased a million of degrees of essential glory, and got laurels upon laurels, crowns upon crowns, and trophies without number. And, unfortunate wretch as I am, I have lost all this eternally, for mere sloth, for want of a little striving for it. Am I not worthy to undergo the pains I suffer, though they were a thousand times more rigorous and intolerable"? I do not wonder that divines affirm this heart-breaking to be far worse than the privation of the sight of God: for to this they can find some ease and comfort; but the other is altogether inconsolable, since it is purely through their own faults.

You may imagine all the virtues to come in upon this; and either voluntarily, or by a sweet kind of violence, to set upon these captive souls, with a new and fierce storm of reproaches.

Faith. If you believed there was a Purgatory indeed, miserable creature! why did you not live so as to avoid its cruel torments?

Hope. If you aimed to gain Paradise, why did you play the fool, so as to amuse yourself with such trifles, and to lose so much precious time in them?

Charity. Oh, how well have you deserved to burn in these flames, since you often scorned to burn with mine, and to serve God with a-heart all inflamed with divine fire; burn, then, at leisure, and die here for shame; since there was a time, thou wouldst neither live nor die with sacred and holy love.

Penance. Is it you that were so frightened with

my rigours, so terrified with my sweet austerities, with which I would have preserved you from these cruel torments? Tell me now, where are your damask beds, your soft quilts, your down pillows, your fine sheets, that were smoother and whiter than milk and cream? your sweet bags and perfumes, all your dainties, all your vanities, all that modish attire and bravery,* which did so besot and enchant you? One sigh, one tear, one act of self-denial, would have kept you out of this place of torments; answer me now, and let me hear what you have to say for yourself.

Prudence. Foolish and senseless soul! how came you so to lose your wits, and even common sense too ; as, knowing the rigour of these flames, to use no caution to prevent them? Oh, how well are these horrid punishments bestowed! This vile creature was so simple, as to believe, that continually offending God, without making Him amends for it in an honourable way, she should pass scot-free, and supply for all with a slight *peccavi*, and so enter into heaven. What folly was this? As if it were a sufficient pretence to be wicked and rebellious, because God is full of mercy. Sit still, then, at the daily task of thy sufferings, and rather think of doubling them : for it is meet that God should show Himself to be God, as well by justice as by mercy; and that both these divine attributes should play their parts in their turns.

Fortitude. How oft have I offered my service to strengthen you, O you careless and lazy soul! how oft have I offered to lend you my arm, my heart, and all my invincible power, to support and bolster up

* *i.e.* Rich and attractive dress.

your faint-heartedness and weakness; and you have disdained to employ it! now, when you are forced to bear the heavy burthen of God's just vengeance, have I not just reason to withdraw my assistance?

Temperance. I told you as much, long since; that, for want of bridling your unruly passions, the time would come when you would curse the hours of all your excesses and disorders, without having power to redeem them but by excessive torments. Do you expect now, inconsiderate soul, that I should pour out water upon your flames; you that have ever slighted me?

Thus all the holy choir of God's darlings, the innocent virtues, come one after another, and beat upon this anvil, laying whole loads of most heavy strokes upon this miserable soul: so that you cannot well imagine what more grievous fortune can befall her: insomuch that the soul, so oppressed with evils, and so furiously battered on all sides with a fresh supply of torments, is forced to cry out: "Miserable that I am, and a thousand times miserable! am I not wretched enough, but must the virtues themselves join their forces with my frailties, to persecute me, and complete my misery? How long, alas! how long will you thus cruelly combine to undo me? you, love, and you, grief; you, by a thousand sweets, and you, by a thousand severities; you, by flattering my pains, and you, by redoubling them; you, by showing me life, and you, by showing me death; you, by estranging me from Paradise, and you, by conducting me to the very gates of hell; you, by sweet expostulations, and you, by bitter reproaches, which go to my very heart? How long, I say once more, will you be so cruelly kind, as to join your forces to imbitter the martyrdom of a poor creature, now grown to be the most miserable wretch under heaven? Forbear; at length, forbear! it is not fit the severity of God's justice should eclipse all the rays of His infinite mercy!"

All were lost,* if the opinion of some were true, who will needs have the devils play the executioners in Purgatory. Lord, what a terrible war would these wicked apostates raise against the holy souls, who are, ere long, to take possession of the places which they have lost in heaven! With what a rage would they assault them, and wreak their barbarous fury upon them, were they to be treated at their mercy! But I had rather follow the opinion of others,† who, with far more reason, methinks, believe that the devils have no power to do them the least mischief. Tell me, what good would they get by it? since the souls can neither offend God, nor lose Paradise; which is the only butt against which the devils level their whole malice. Origen fancied‡ the devil to be so sullenly proud, that having been once foiled by a soul, he will never after come near it, nor have anything more to do with it. If this be so, the devils will beware how they come near Purgatory, where there are so many victorious souls. Besides, we may

* *i.e.* We should, indeed, have reached the most terrible consideration which the thought of Purgatory could furnish.

† St. Thomas, in 4, d. 20 et 21 ; Suarez, d. 46, sec. 3.

‡ The author rightly puts this opinion among the "fancies' of that great but erring mind.

suppose that God will not permit it ; nor can we see what good can arise thence to God's glory. Possibly,. also, these punishments which the devils would inflict,. might shorten the term of the soul's durance ; and this may be the cause why they are loth to meddle with them, lest they send them so much the sooner into heaven. However, some of the learned* think that these souls, bordering so near upon hell, may very probably see the devils and the damned souls,. and hear their most execrable blasphemies ; and that this is no small addition to their pains, to hear their good God, whom they entirely love, to be incessantly cursed, blasphemed, and renounced by those devilish and sacrilegious spirits. St. Catharine of Siena was heard to say, she had rather suffer all the torments of hell, than hear one blasphemy against God, for whom she had so much cordial love, and who is of Himself so lovely. I confess, this is a sweet kind of torment, as proceeding from supernatural and divine love ; but I maintain,. withal, that it is a torment, and a most grievous one : because, though the arrows of love are gilded over, or made of pure gold, yet they are as. sharp-pointed, and as piercing to the quick, as those of grief, though they be of steel.

Confusion is one of the most intolerable evils which can befall a soul : and therefore St. Paul,† speaking of our Blessed Saviour, insists much upon this, that He had the courage, and the love for us all, to overcome: the pain of a horrible confusion, which doubtless is an insupportable evil, to a man of intelligence and courage. Tell me, then, if you can, what a burning

* Suarez, sec. n. 10.   † Heb. xii. 2.

shame, and what a terrible confusion it must needs be to those noble and generous souls, to behold themselves overwhelmed with a confused chaos of fire, and such a base fire, which affords no other light but a sullen glimmering, choked up with a sulphureous and stinking smoke, and in the interim to know that the souls of many country clowns, mere idiots, poor women and simple religious persons, go straight up to heaven, whilst they lie there burning : they, that were so knowing, so rich, and so wise ; they that were councillors to kings, eminent preachers of God's Word, and renowned oracles in the world ; they that were so great divines, so great statesmen, so capable of high employments. This confusion is much heightened by their further knowing how easily they might have avoided all this, and would not. Sometimes they would have given whole mountains of gold, to be rid of a stone in the kidneys, or a fit of the gout, colic, or burning fever. And for a handful of silver they might have redeemed many years' torments in that fiery furnace ; and, alas! they chose rather to give it to their dogs and their horses, and sometimes to men more beasts than they, and much more unworthy. Methinks, this thought must be more vexing than the fire itself, though never so grievous.

And yet there remains one thought more, which certainly has a great share in completing their martyrdom : and that is, the remembrance of their children or heirs, which they left behind them ; who swim in nectar and live jollily on the goods which they purchased with the sweat of their brows, and yet are so ungrateful, so brutish, and so barbarous that they will scarce vouchsafe to say a *Pater noster* in a whole month for their souls who brought them into the world; and who, to place them in a terrestial paradise of all worldly delights, made a hard venture of their own souls, and had like to have exchanged a temporal punishment for an eternal. The remnants and superfluities of their lackeys, a throw of dice, and yet less than that, might have set them free from these hellish torments; and these wicked, ungrateful wretches would not so much as think on it.

§ 4.—*How long the souls are detained in Purgatory.*

If all these punishments passed away like a tempest; if the time of their continuance were but short; their case were not so deplorable. But how long, think you, does a soul dwell in Purgatory? First, it is most certain, that these pains are not eternal; otherwise it were not Purgatory, but hell itself: for in this chiefly lies the difference between hell and Purgatory, that the pains of Purgatory last but for a time; those of hell, for an eternity. Again, it is most certain, that they survive not the Day of Judgment; and St. Augustine* proves it evidently: because then all souls are to receive their last doom, and be immoveably fixed in an eternity of good or evil. Thirdly, it is most certain, that all the souls shall not be there punished equally, neither for extent of time, nor proportion of torment: for, as their crimes were not equal, so the punishment cannot be equal, where justice

St. Augustine, *De Civit.* c. 16.

D

bears the sway. Fourthly: It is also certain, says the learned and judicious Suarez,* after others, that we must not apply the revelations of certain devout persons, to all the souls in Purgatory; but rather ought to be very reserved in this kind, and not easily to give credit to all such stories which pass for revelations : for though God, in His secret judgments, may be pleased to punish some disloyal souls after a particular manner, yet must we take heed how we draw general conclusions from particular cases. For since private revelations are not articles of faith, we must be very cautious, and proceed warily in this matter; especially where we see such kind of revelations seemingly to clash one against another. We must therefore pass by such extraordinary cases, and honour them with due respect; but not build so much upon them as to draw thence universal maxims. Wherefore in this place I mean not to speak but of the common and ordinary style of God's providence ; laying aside all particular visions, and personal exemplary punishments, which God has reserved to Himself. Now, there have been some so bold as to maintain that all the souls lie in Purgatory but a few hours, and are then quit and released of their pains. Their grounds are : first, because the pains may be so doubled, and screwed up to such a height, as to equal any extension of pain whatsoever. Secondly, because the souls there do exercise such acts of love, and other sublime virtues, all which conspire to purify these poor creatures, so that the business is soon despatched. Were this true, it were very good news; but the

* Suarez, d. 46, sec. 4, n. 6.

mischief is, that most divines censure this assertion as too bold and temerarious : and, in truth, it has very little or no probability, and were a way in effect* to destroy Purgatory; since we may cut off half of those few hours they speak of, by redoubling the pains, and another half of these by redoubling them again, and so go on, still halving the time, by doubling the pains, till we reduce them to a quarter of an hour, or half a quarter, or possibly to an instant, or so little durance as to be scarce begun but ended. Which kind of Purgatory, though it may be the case with those souls which depart immediately before the Day of Judgment, when the intensity of the pain must supply for the extent of time, which will be then wanting, forasmuch there is to be no more Purgatory after that general accounting Day—yet to apply it commonly to other souls, where there is no need of such subtilities, would be confounding all things. It is the ordinary course of God's justice to proceed by degrees; and, therefore, there must be a competent time allotted for those punishments. And this is the general belief of the Church, that the souls are kept there for a time, some more, some less, each one according to his desert; and though perhaps some choice souls do but, as it were, kiss the gates of Purgatory, and rather feel the smoke than the fire, yet the greater part of them lie there for some considerable time, to satisfy the sweet rigour of Divine justice. I am not ignorant that some great divines have believed, that if a soul stay there for a year or two, it is all. For, say they, how can you require more of them than to be **two** years

i. e. Would be, in fact, a method to destroy, etc.

D 2

miserably tormented in a burning furnace? That which here might have been redeemed with a tear of true contrition, or with a sigh of ardent charity, can it not be purged with flames of fire in two whole years in the other world? The most barbarous cruelty in this life is scarce ever seen to reach beyond a few hours: and what shall we then say of two years in Purgatory, which are, as it were, two ages, or two little eternities, so great are the torments. Shall it not be enough to purify the most unclean soul in the world, so she be in the state of grace? But yet this opinion is not received in the Church; and it is a great madness to attempt anything contrary to the common judgment of the Church and her learned Doctors.

Sotus held a singular opinion of his own;* that no soul remains in Purgatory above ten years. For, said he, we must set some bounds to the rigour of God's justice, who doth all things in number, weight, and measure, and is said to dispose all things sweetly. And is not ten years of most bitter pains a great number, a grievous weight, and an overflowing measure? to say nothing of so many prayers, so many Masses, so many tears, so many privileged altars, and plenary Indulgences; so many alms and other good deeds of the living; and then the most powerful intercession of the whole Court of Heaven, but especially of our Blessed Lady, and her Beloved Son, who is the Attorney-General of the whole Church, and who pleads for it with His most persuasive and divine rhetoric. Yet for all this, I must

* Sec. in 4, d. 17, q. 3.

tell you, many divines lay heavy censures upon this
opinion, not hesitating to call it, not only temerarious
but also erroneous; and the common sense of the
Church is quite contrary, as appears by the imme-
morial custom of perpetual foundations of set Masses,
to be yearly said, for such particular persons, and to
continue to the world's end; all which would be
needless, if Almighty God put a period to their
punishments after ten years; for to what purpose
are those Masses after the ten years are expired?
And, though the most learned of this age will not
take upon them to condemn this opinion as erroneous,
yet they all accuse it of much temerity; because, in
truth, this whole business is very uncertain, as being
a secret locked up in the cabinet of God Himself,
and letters sealed up, which our Saviour would not
hitherto open to His Spouse the Church; so that,
whilst it remains in the nature of a secret, we must
not presume to define anything precisely. Only, this
we know, that many souls do but touch Purgatory, as
it were with their finger, and away; others lie there
whole hours, days, months, and years: and, as we
are not easily to credit those visions, which threaten
the souls in Purgatory, with a continuance of their
torments until the last Day, so are we to believe
that God can well punish some of them so long,
that the space of ten years, in comparison, should
seem little or nothing to it. Hence it is a very
laudable and pious custom to found Masses in
perpetuity; because, alas, who knows whether he
may not be of the number of those unfortunate
souls who are to be kept there so long? How few

know truly the state of their own souls, and the
debts they are to pay to the severity of our most
just Judge! He is, indeed, full of clemency; but
such as is ever accompanied with an impartial
justice, worthy of God. I may add here, that the
piety of the founders looks not only upon the releasing of their own souls out of torments, which they
are assured will have an end sooner or later; but
they open their hearts and bowels of charity, and
extend it to others, who from time to time shall be
in Purgatory, and, very possibly, have nobody to
remember them in their devotions. This certainly
is a work of charity, well becoming a good Catholic,
and a well-disposed soul; to provide so as to cooperate, even after his death, to the help and salvation of other souls: and to be ever and anon
sending some into heaven, by antedating the time
of their deliverance, and increasing the number of
the glorious Saints. Meantime, what an inconsolable grief is it to the poor souls to see themselves
plunged, over head and ears, in flames of fire; and
condemned to remain there ten, twenty, a hundred
years, and perhaps to the world's end, if their friends
upon earth do not afford them their best assistance?

There are some few of late, are fallen so far into the
contrary extreme, that they cannot afford that a soul,
once in Purgatory, should ever get out before the Day
of Judgment. But as this strange paradox took its
rise chiefly from a false apprehension of the nature
of a spiritual substance, and other wild principles of
a newly minted philosophy, so is it generally cried
down, and contradicted by many known apparitions

and revelations, which the reader will meet with in this treatise ; attested by such weighty authors and Fathers of the Church, that he has little reason to suspect them for old wives' tales or melancholy dreams, as these men would have them. It seems, moreover, to have been blasted long ago, and condemned in a particular Bull of Pope Benedict XI., and in the holy Council of Florence;* where it was expressly defined, that "those souls which, after they have contracted the blemish of sin, are" purged "either in their bodies, or being unclothed of their bodies, are" presently "received into heaven." And since the author of this extravagance will have tradition to be the sole rule of our faith (of which tradition we have no clearer proof than from the testimony of the Church), let him but look into the general doctrine and practice of the Church, both now at this present, and time out of mind, and he shall discover as clear a tradition for this common persuasion of the souls being released out of Purgatory, some sooner, some later, according to their own deserts, and the relief of our suffrages, as for any other thing in the world. Do not good people generally ground themselves upon this, when they offer up their prayers, give alms, procure Masses and dirges, apply Indulgences, for the present relief of their deceased friends? Is not the whole practice of Christians, in all that concerns their piety to the faithful departed, built so wholly upon this, that were it not true, we must conclude that the whole Catholic Church has been all along fooled by her

* In *Bullar. Rom.* Conc. Flor. in lit. Unionis, art. 4.

pastors and doctors? Who has ever hitherto so much as fancied it in a dream, that his suffrages for the dead were to be of no greater advantage to them, than so far forth as they had power to advance the time appointed for the Day of Judgment? which, for my part, I apprehend so coldly, that, did I not rely upon better motives, I should soon lay aside all devotion for the souls departed.

But I mean not here to dispute the question; since this treatise is not intended so much in a polemical, as in an affectuous and moving way. And therefore I leave it for others, who have already entered the lists, and are engaged in the quarrel. And so I take no notice, how it may consist with God's impartial justice, that, whereas many souls may leave this world in the same condition as to Purgatory, that is, in this author's opinion, with the same burden of depraved affections, some of them shall lie a thousand years in Purgatory; to wit, those that die a thousand years before the Day of Judgment; and others but a day, or an hour, or a moment; to wit, those that die immediately before that general reckoning Day. For, since he acknowledges no other pain in Purgatory but that which flows from the said crooked inclinations and affections bent against reason, which I suppose to be the same in all; why should some of them (as must necessarily follow on these principles) shake them off so soon, and others groan so long under them? Again, I say nothing how harshly it sounds in a Christian's ear that a holy soul in the other world should not only still pursue the same wicked inclinations, for example, to drunkenness, gluttony, and carnality, which it had in this life, but that this should be its only punishment. Neither do I say how, in this opinion, great sinners, that die immediately after baptism (who certainly go directly into heaven), must needs carry their Purgatory with them into heaven.* For, since it is evident that baptism does not blot out their perverse inclinations, they cannot be dispossessed of them, but must of necessity carry them into the other world, as well as others ; and consequently must have their Purgatory in Heaven : Purgatory being nothing else, in this author's opinion, but the inherent strife and fury of such irrational affections. I pass by a world of other absurdities : because my aim, as I told you, in publishing this treatise, is not to canvass curious and impertinent questions of Purgatory, but to move the reader to a solid devotion for the poor souls, which I fear is not a little cooled since these fond opinions came to light.

But now, methinks, I hear my reader very inquisitive to know

§ 5.—*Whether their pains grow less and less.*

It is pity to see, sometimes, how your greatest divines are entangled, and lost in their over-subtle speculations. As for the pain of loss, which the souls endure by being deprived of the sight of God, they agree that it is daily much lessened ; for, seeing the time draw nearer, in which they are to be made happy with the sight of God, whom they love so ardently, it exceed-

* Trid. Sess. 14, c. 2 ; Flor. Act. 4. cit.

ingly rejoices them, and certainly cannot but much
sweeten, and consequently lessen their pains, by the
frequent repetitions of that devout aspiration, which
St. Teresa was wont to use, when she heard the clock
strike : "O lovely hour, how dost thou rejoice me, by
bringing me the welcome news, that I am now a whole
hour nearer to the sight of God!" For a heart that
loves cannot but be overjoyed to know that he ap-
proaches to the fair Object of his love, though it be
but a moment nearer. But as for the pain of sense,
your Doctors are divided ; some hold, that, as regards
the continuance, that is certainly shortened every day
by the day which is past, which is evident; and in
particular, that the prayers of the faithful obtain from
God an abridgment of the length of the time which
He assigned for their punishment ; so that, the more
one prays for the souls, the more is cut off of the time
of their suffering, which by that means becomes the
more tolerable. But as for the sharpness and intense-
ness of the pain, and the action or activity of the fire,
that is as grievous in the last moment as at the first,
and as painful in the end as at the beginning of their
Purgatory. And they would comfort the souls hereby,
as if this were best for them ; because the greater the
pains are which they endure, the sooner are they
purged, and made worthy to enjoy the presence of
God. Others teach, that both the pain and the time
are continually lessened, according to the proportion
of the relief which they receive from the suffrages of
the Church. And why not? since God's goodness is
so great, such is the desire of the Church that begs it,
and the tears of the faithful pretend to no less ; and

we must not consider the fire as an element working naturally, and equally at all times, but rather as an instrument of God's justice, who gives it more or less force and power to work upon the souls as He pleases. Why should Almighty God, who is so loving a Father, refuse to give this relief, at the earnest suit of children, in behalf of their parents, brothers, sisters, and dearest friends; I say, at their instance, who are so sensible of their torments, and so much concerned for their ease and relief? I willingly embrace this opinion, as more worthy of the bowels of mercy, more sympathizing with the Heart of Christ Jesus, and better suiting with the prayers of the Church, and the sighs of Christians. And certainly, none can better clear this difficulty than the souls themselves who feel the pains we speak of; and these have often, by God's permission, appeared to their friends and devout persons, and borne witness for this truth, that their pains were still lessened, as they received new succour from the pious endeavours of their friends upon earth; until they came at last to cease, and reach their term. And we must not here be too nice and hard of belief; for, as it is an argument of too much rashness and folly, to give credit to all pretended visions, of what nature soever, so it argues too much brutishness and profaneness to believe none; especially when they are authorized by the Church, and by persons of authority and credit beyond exception: so that we must either believe them, or believe nothing in this world.

§ 6.—*A notable example in confirmation of all the preceding doctrine.*

Before I leave off finishing this picture, or put a period to the representation of the pains of Purgatory, I cannot but relate a very remarkable history, which will be as a living picture before your eyes. But be sure you take it not to be of the number of those idle stories which pass for old wives' tales, or mere imaginations of cracked brains and simple souls. No : I will tell you nothing but what Venerable Bede, so grave an author, witnesses to have happened in his time, and to have been generally believed all over England, without contradiction ; and to have been the cause of wonderful effects : and which is so authentical that Cardinal Bellarmine, a man of such judgment as the world knows, having related it himself, concludes thus : "For my part I firmly believe this history, as very conformable to the Holy Scripture, and whereof I can have no doubt without wronging truth, and wounding my own conscience, which ought readily to yield assent unto that which is attested by so many and so credible witnesses, and confirmed by such holy and admirable events."

About the year of our Lord 690, a certain Englishman, in the county of Northumberland, by name Brithelmus, being dead for a time, was conducted to the place of Purgatory by a guide, whose countenance and apparel was full of light : you may imagine it was his good angel. Here he was shown two broad valleys of a vast and infinite length, one full of glowing firebrands and terrible flames, the other as full of hail, ice, and snow; and in both these were innumerable souls, who, as with a whirlwind, were tossed up and down out of the intolerable scorching flames, into the insufferable rigours of cold, and out of these into those again, without a moment of repose or respite. This he took to be hell, so frightful were those torments; but his good angel told him no, it was Purgatory, where the souls did penance for their sins, and especially such as had deferred their conversion until the hour of death · and that many of them were set free before the Day of Judgment, for the good prayers, alms, and fasts of the living, and chiefly by the holy Sacrifice of the Mass. Now this holy man, being raised again from death to life by the power of God, first made a faithful relation of all that he had seen, to the great amaze-ment of the hearers, then retired himself into the church, and spent the whole night in prayer; and soon after, gave away his whole estate, partly to his wife and children, partly to the poor, and taking upon him the habit and profession of a monk, led so austere a life, that even if his tongue had been silent, yet his life and conversation spake aloud what wonders he had seen in the other world. Sometimes they would see him, old as he was, in freezing water up to the ears, praying and singing with much sweetness and in-credible fervour; and if they asked him: "Brother, alas! how can you suffer so much sharp and biting cold?" "O my friends," would he say, "I have seen other manner of cold than this." Thus, when he even groaned under the voluntary burden of a world of most cruel mortifications, and was questioned how it was possible for a weak and broken body like his to undergo such austerities, "Alas, my dear brethren," would he still say, "I have seen far greater austerities than these : they are but roses and perfumes in comparison of what I have seen in the subterraneous lakes of Purgatory." And in these kinds of austerities he spent the remainder of his life, and made a holy end, and purchased an eternal Paradise, for having had but a sight of the pains of Purgatory. And we, dear Christians, if we believed in good earnest, or could but once procure to have a true sight or apprehension of them, should certainly have other thoughts, and live in another fashion, than we do.

THE SECOND SURVEY.

A GLIMPSE OF THE PARADISE OF PURGATORY, OR OF
THE INEFFABLE JOYS AND HEAVENLY CONSOLATIONS
OF THE SOULS THERE.

I DO not style that the Paradise of Purgatory which
some have fancied, as if the souls, having almost clean
cancelled out all those impurities which they here contracted, were to be conveyed into a terrestrial Paradise
or a most delicious garden of pleasure, smiling with a
divine amenity, there to dispose themselves the better
to see God, without suffering any pain of sense. For,
although this fancy may appear to have something of
piety, yet has it little or nothing of solidity ; and I am
resolved to lay down nothing here that is not very
massive, solid, and substantially well grounded. Now,
the Council of Florence * seems to take away all
credit from this opinion of a terrestrial Paradise ; and
so, down goes all that goodly fabric built in the air.
For, says the Council, either the souls are quite
purged, and if so, they are immediately received
into heaven, and made worthy to behold God ; or
they want still more purging and refining, and then
they are still like to lie by it in Purgatory. From
whence it clearly follows, that the souls departed can
have no time left them to entertain themselves in
those ' pleasant gardens and sweet breathings, which
these so much magnify.

* Flor. Sess. ult.

Wherefore, under the notion of the Paradise of Purgatory, I understand the excessive joys of these captive souls, the incomparable acts of their will and understanding, and the continual favours showered down upon them from heaven, even amidst their most cruel torments.

§ 1.—*How these excessive joys can be consistent with their unspeakable torments.*

To make this good, we must first suppose that the actions of a soul disengaged from the body are quite of a different nature from those which she exercises while she is chained to a lump of flesh, drowned in blood and other humours, kept in thraldom by her tyrannical passions and brutish affections, overburdened with deadly frights and fears, and leading a kind of slavish and miserable life. Tertullian came near the mark, when he compared a soul in this world to a coachman that is to guide four unruly horses without reins; a soldier that has his sword in his hands but his arms tied; a swift courser that would run but is tethered; a bird that would fly, but has his wings clammed up with bird-lime. Now, when the soul is once set free from this bondage, and lives at liberty, this coachman drives, this soldier strikes, this courser runs, this bird flies, and this soul does what she pleases, without control. Besides, that which makes the actions of a soul in this life to be so weak and imperfect is the necessary dependance which she has on the body, into which she is so· ingrafted that she seems to be but one and the self-same thing with it. If the body be oppressed with pain, the soul is so deeply plunged in it, she can think of nothing else; you must work a miracle to make her have so much as a good thought or give you a good word; she is grown so lumpish, you would think her whole spirit were resolved into flesh. And this may be the reason why the Holy Scripture so often compares men to beasts; as, to lions, foxes, and the like : because their souls become brutish, by following the dictates and motions of their sensual and animal appetites.

But you must observe, that all this happens while a soul is left to herself, and her own natural strength; for when the Divine Goodness is pleased to furnish her with plenty of grace even in this world, as wicked as it is, this grace has such an ascendancy over nature, and breathes such spirit and vigour into a soul, that she can wrestle with all difficulties, and remove all obstacles; nay, though the body be borne down and sunk into the very centre of misery, yet can she still hold up her head, and steer her course towards heaven.

Now, would you clearly see how the souls can at the same instant swim in a paradise of delights and yet be overwhelmed with the hellish torments of Purgatory? Cast your eyes upon the holy martyrs of God's Church, and observe their behaviour. They were torn, mangled, dismembered, flayed alive, racked, broiled, burnt—and tell me, was not this to live in a kind of hell? And yet, in the very height of their torments their hearts and souls were ready to leap for joy; you would have taken them to be already trans-

E

ported into heaven. Hear them but speak for themselves. "O lovely cross," cried out St. Andrew,
"made beautiful by the precious Body of Christ, how
long have I desired thee, and with what care have
I sought thee! and now, that I have found thee,
receive me into thy arms, and lift me up to my dear
Redeemer. O death,* how amiable art thou in my
eyes, and how sweet is thy cruelty!" "Your coals,"
said St. Cecily, "your flaming firebrands, and all the
terrors of death, are to me but as so many fragrant
roses and lilies, sent from heaven." "Shower down
upon me," cried St. Stephen, "whole deluges of stones,
whilst I see the heavens open and Jesus Christ standing at the right Hand of His Eternal Father, to behold
the fidelity of His champion." "Turn," exclaimed
St. Laurence, "oh, turn, the other side, thou cruel
tyrant! this is already broiled, and cooked fit for thy
palate. Oh, how well am I pleased to suffer this
little purgatory for the love of my Saviour." "Make
haste, O my soul," cried St. Agnes, "to cast thyself
upon the bed of flames which thy dear Spouse has
prepared for thee." "Oh," cried St. Felicitas, and
the mother of the Machabees, "oh, that I had a
thousand children, or a thousand lives, to sacrifice
them all to my God. What a pleasure it is to suffer
for so good a cause!" "Welcome tyrants, tigers,
lions," writes St. Ignatius the Martyr; "let all the
torments that the devils can invent come upon me,
so I may enjoy my Saviour. I am the wheat of
Christ; oh, let me be ground with the lions' teeth.

* From the author's text, it seems doubtful whether this
sentence is to be attributed to St. Andrew or to St. Cæcilia.

Now I begin indeed to be the disciple of Christ."
"Oh, the happy stroke of a sword," might St. Paul
well exclaim, "that no sooner cuts off my head, but
it makes a breach for my soul to enter into heaven.
Let it be far from me to glory in anything, but in the
Cross of our Lord Jesus Christ. Let all evils band
against me, and let my body be never so overloaded
with afflictions, the joy of my heart will be sure to have
the mastery, and my soul will be still replenished with
such heavenly consolations that no words, nor even
thoughts, are able to express it."

You may imagine, then, that the souls, once un-
fettered from the body, may, together with their
torments, be capable of great comforts and divine
favours, and break forth into resolute, heroical and
even supercelestial acts. The Holy Ghost tells us,
that "the corruptible body is a load upon the soul,
and the earthly habitation presseth down the mind
that museth upon many things."* So that a soul, by
the infirmities of the body, is violently kept from
the free exercise of her functions; whereas, if the
body were supple, pliable, and willing to follow the
persuasions of a resolute and generous soul, or the
inspirations with which she is plentifully supplied from
above, what might we not be able to do, even in this
life? Now, that which is not done here, but by very
few, who are looked upon as so many miracles and
prodigies of men, is easily performed by those sepa-
rate holy souls, who are in the very porch of heaven,
assured of their salvation. Lastly; would you have
a most perfect exemplar and idea of this wonderful

* Wisdom ix. 15.

E 2

combination of joys and griefs in one single person?
You may clearly see it in the most sacred Person of
our Blessed Saviour; who, in the midst of His bitter
Passion, and in the very height of His Agony and
extreme dereliction, when He not only seemed to
have been abandoned by His Eternal Father, but had
even abandoned and forsaken Himself, by miraculously withholding the superior part of His blessed
Soul from relieving and assisting the inferior, yet even
then, had all the comforts of heaven, and saw God
face to face, and consequently, was at the self-same
time most happy, by the fruition of the beatifical
vision : and yet so oppressed with griefs, that He
cried out Himself, " My Soul is sorrowful unto death;"
and again, "O My God, alas ! why hast Thou thus
forsaken Me !"   Conceive something like unto this,
of the souls in Purgatory, who are most miserably
tormented, and yet replenished with heavenly comforts.

§ 2.—*Two grounds of their comforts ; the double
assurance they have: of their salvation, and
impeccability.*

The better to unfold you this riddle, I must tell
you, that possibly the most solid and powerful ground
of their comfort, is the assurance of their eternal
salvation, and that one day, when it shall please God,
they shall have their part in the joys of Paradise.
That which is the sorest affliction in this life, unto the
most refined souls, in the greatest torments, is the
fear of offending God, and making an unhappy end,

for want of the gift of perseverance; of which none can be assured without a particular revelation; and so becoming the devil's martyrs, by purchasing one hell with another. For, if an angel should come down from heaven, and give this infallible assurance unto an afflicted person, that undoubtedly he shall be saved, as being one of the choice number of the elect, certainly his very heart would leap for joy; nor would the severest usage, with death itself, and death represented in her most frightful and ghastly attire, seem cruel or irksome unto him, but exceeding welcome and pleasant. When Almighty God was pleased once to reveal unto St. Francis His eternal predestination, and to seal him, as it were, a deed of gift of Paradise, this seraph incarnate was so transported with an ecstasy of joy, and so ravished out of himself, that for eight days together he did nothing but go up and down, crying out: "Paradise, Paradise! O my soul, thou shalt have Paradise!" and had so quite lost all memory of eating, drinking, sleeping, suffering, living, dying, and all things else, as being inebriated with the sweet remembrance of that comfortable news of eternal bliss, that he was not at all sensible of any oppression of nature, nor seemed to be the least concerned for it. For, said he, what can anything else signify to me, since I am one day to have Paradise, with all the delights of heaven? Now, if we credit the holy Doctors of the Church, and best divines of the Christian world, the souls in Purgatory are most certain of their salvation.* For no sooner is the soul departed this life, but she is brought to a

* Suarez, d. 47, sec. 3.

particular judgment, where she receives an award of
her eternal state of glory, or confusion; and from the
mouth of God hears the irrevocable sentence from
which there is no appeal, no civil request, no review
of process, no writ of error: for this decree of God's
justice must immediately be put in execution. They
say, further, that in the same moment that a soul sees
herself condemned to Purgatory, she sees also the
precise time prescribed her to continue there, according to the ordinary course of God's justice. But
whether she know also, by Divine revelation, who
will pray for her, and what assistance in particular
they will give her, or how much will be cut off, of the
time determined for her punishment, is a nicer question,
which I purposely leave untouched for others to exercise their wits in, as they please: I make haste to
take up the thread of my discourse that I was letting
fall; in which I am to lay before your eyes the ineffable joys of the souls in Purgatory, when they seriously
reflect upon the certainty of their salvation, and how
soon they shall be drowned in the Divinity, and yet
swim in an ocean of all heavenly comforts. When
Jacob knew for certain that he was to have the fair
Rachel, he was content to be espoused first to Lia,
though she was blear-eyed, and ill-favoured; and,
besides, a world of heats and colds, frights and fears,
and fourteen years' toilsome service, seemed scarce an
hour to him : so much was his heart enchanted with a
holy love of his dearly beloved Rachel; and so true
it is, that for the enjoyment of that which a soul loves
in good earnest, she makes no reckoning of fire and
flames, and a thousand Purgatories. So that a soul

that is confident of one day espousing Rachel, that is,
the Church triumphant, objects not to be first espoused
to Lia, that is, the Church suffering, with all the pains
in Purgatory, so long as it shall please God; and
fourteen years are unto her but as an hour; such is
the excess of her love to heaven. "Oh, with what a
good heart do I drink up my tears," said the royal
Prophet,* "when I remember I shall pass into the
heavenly tabernacle! were I to make my passage
thither through hell itself, how willingly would I
run that way?" And to the same tune cried out
St. Chrysostom, with a masculine voice, and a heart
which was all heart: "If I were to pass through a
thousand hells, so I might in the end of all meet with
Paradise and my God, how pleasing would these
hells seem unto me!" And certainly, there are infinite
souls who would be ready to sign it with their heart-
blood, that they would be willing to dwell in the
flames of Purgatory till the Day of Judgment, upon
condition of being sure of eternal glory at the last;
for, believe it, they that know well the meaning of
these four words, God, Eternity, Glory, and Security,
cannot but have a moderate apprehension of Purgatory
fire, be it never so hot and furious.

Another heavenly comfort which rejoices these
happy souls in the midst of their torments, is an
infallible and certain assurance which they have, that,
although their pains be never so insupportable, yet
shall they never offend God, neither mortally nor
venially; nor show the least sign of impatience or
indignation. A true lover of God understands this

* Psalm xli. 3, 4.

language; and, if he do not, he shall in a moment
learn it in Purgatory, and find by experience that a
soul there, had rather be plunged into the deepest
pit of hell, than be guilty of the least voluntary
misdemeanour. So that, seeing herself to be grown
impeccable, and that no evils can have the power to
make her offend God, and that all impatience dies at the
gates of Purgatory, from whence all sins and human
failings are quite banished—O God, what a solid comfort
must this needs be unto her ! The greatest affliction
that good people can have in the sufferings of this
life, is the fear of offending God, or to think that the
violence of their torments may make them subject to
break out into a thousand foolish expressions, and to
toss in their heads many foolish thoughts, filling their
imaginations with a world of chimeras, and idle
fancies, or frightful objects ; or, in a word, because
they apprehend either death, or sin, or the loss of their
merit and labour, or that God is angry with them.
For grief, with the devil's help, strives to snatch out
of our hands the victorious palm of our sufferings, or
at least to make us stoop to some frailties and imperfections, which imbitter our hearts. And were it not
for this just fear, Saints would not fear the greatest
evils they can endure in this world. What a joy, then,
must it be to these holy innocent souls, to see themselves become altogether impeccable ! The reason of
this is clear ; because, the particular judgment being
once over, the final sentence is also pronounced, and
the soul is no longer in a capacity to merit or demerit,
nor so much as to satisfy, by any voluntary sufferings
of her own ; but only to submit to the sweet rigour

of God's justice, who has assigned such a proportion
of pains, answerable to her demerits, and so to clear
her conscience, and blot out the remainder of her
frailties and impurities. Make haste * to do well
before death, is the counsel of Almighty God; for the
appointed time wherein to heap up treasures of justice
and merits is, before you appear in judgment; for
after that, it will be too late. The very instant that a
soul leaves the body, according to God's law, there is
no more time for merit or demerit; and therefore the
souls that are sent into Purgatory are most certain they
shall never more commit the least sin that can be
imagined. When St. Anthony was so furiously
assaulted with a whole rabble regiment of devils,
he was not greatly daunted at all their hideous shapes,
terrible howlings, and rude blows; all his fear was
of offending God: he apprehended more the strokes
of impatience than all the wounds of hell; he called
upon Christ for help, and having obtained the favour
of a personal visit, he made Him this loving complaint and sweet expostulation.

"O good Jesus! where were you, alas, where were
you even now, my dear Saviour, when your emenies
and mine conspired so cruelly against me? why came
you no sooner to relieve me?" "I was here," replied
Christ, "beholding thee, and preserving thy heart
from sin." "If it be so," said the invincible hermit,
"do but assure me this, that I shall not sin, and let
Lucifer, with all his accursed crew and hellish power,
nay, let all the world besides, band against me! Since
my God stands by me, and will secure me from

* Eccles. ix. 10.

offending Him, I make nothing of all the rest. Pain
is no more pain; hell is no more a hell, but a mere
paradise; since it helps me to gain Paradise, which is
worthy to be purchased with a million of hells."

§ 3.—*More grounds of comfort, arising from their voluntary suffering, their disinterested love of God, and exact conformity with His holy will.*

In the next place, take this most sweet and weighty
consideration. An evil that is forced, and against
one's will, is a true evil indeed; the constraint and
violence it carries along with it, imbitters it above
measure, and renders it insupportable : whereas, if
the evil be voluntary, it is a good evil, a lovely evil,
an evil to be purchased at any price. Witness the holy
martyrs of God's Church, who, when they voluntarily
shed their blood, and with a goodwill poured out
their lives for God's cause, though at the cost of the
most inhuman torments imaginable, seemed to make
but little reckoning of the smart of them, as you may
observe by their conduct. For some of them would
put back the worms that were crept out of their
ulcerous sores, others kiss the burning coals, and, by
way of honour, place them on their heads. This
holy martyr embraces the gibbet, as if he took it to
be an easy ladder, whereby to mount up straight into
heaven; another provokes tigers and lions to dis-
member him. This tender virgin leaps into the fire
prepared for her, without staying for the executioner's
help; another casts herself into the sea, to preserve
herself pure. See the force of Christian resolution,

which is steered by Divine maxims. They die, and smile at it; they seem to court death itself; they choose rather to be under the hands of a bloody executioner, who can at most bereave them of their lives, than in the power of the son of an Emperor, who may rob them of the lilies of their virginal integrity. Nothing can be grievous to him that acts vigorously, and suffers voluntarily whatsoever falls in his way. This, then, is one of the souls' chief comforts in those fiery dungeons. They accept their pains, as from the hands of their loving Father, who, out of His paternal care, makes choice of those rough instruments to polish and refine them, and so fit them for His presence. They look upon them as love-tokens sent from their Beloved, and esteem them rather as precious gifts of their loving Lord, than as cruel punishments inflicted by a severe enemy. They kiss the rod, and the Fatherly hand which makes use of it for their sovereign good. When a surgeon makes a deep incision to let out the water of a dropsy; when he strikes his lancet into the arm; when he cut off a gangrened member, the diseased person kisses the hand that made the wound, embraces the surgeon, though sprinkled with his blood, opens his mouth to give thanks, his purse to reward, his eyes to bathe in tears, and his very heart to love cordially this kind murderer, who has so cruelly mishandled him, to do him good, and to save his life. What, think you, is the language of these holy souls, these children of God, in the midst of their severest torments? " Sweet rigours of heaven; loving cruelties! ah, why do you vouchsafe so to humble your greatness, to take the pains to purify us poor creatures, worthy of a thousand hells? Oh, the profuse goodness of the Almighty, who is pleased, with the tenderness of a loving Father, to chastise His wicked servants, and so to adopt them for His dear children! Was it necessary that Himself should take the trouble upon Him to stretch out the hand of His infinite justice, to purify such disloyal souls, far unworthy of a love so cordial? Oh, let Him burn, let Him strike, let Him thunder; it is but reason He should do so; for since He is our Father, our Creator, our Redeemer, our dear All, the sole Object of our lives; howsoever He handles us, we shall still take it for a great favour, and esteem ourselves over-happy to be treated, though never so severely, by so good a Hand. Have they not reason? Believe it, they experience it to be so sweet, and so reasonable; nay, they judge it so necessary for them, to suffer in these flames, that though they should discover a thousand gates open, and a free passage for them to fly out of Purgatory into Paradise, not so much as one soul would stir out before she had fully satisfied the Divine justice. Paradise would be to them a Purgatory, should they carry thither but the least blemish in the world. When Isaac saw the sword in Abraham's hand, ready to strike off his head, and reflected that he was to receive the deadly wound from the hands of his dear father, that good and virtuous young man could neither find tongue to plead for his life, nor feet to run away and decline the stroke, nor hands to defend himself, nor so much as eyes to deplore his sad misfortune; but was content to have a heart to

love his good father, and a head to lose, and a life to sacrifice upon the altar of obedience : and he looked upon the fire which was prepared to destroy him, as the odoriferous flaming pile of the phœnix, wherein she is consumed, to rise again to a new and happy life. The holy souls that burn in the flames of Purgatory, are much better disposed to embrace whatsoever God shall ordain, than Isaac was in regard of his father.

But there is yet something of a higher nature to be said upon this point. We have all the reason in the world to believe that God, of His infinite goodness, inspires these holy souls with a thousand heavenly lights, and such ravishing thoughts, that they cannot but take themselves to be extremely happy : so happy that St. Catharine of Genoa professed she had learnt of Almighty God that, excepting only the blessed Saints in heaven, there were no joys comparable to those of the souls in Purgatory. For, said she, when they consider that they are in the hands of God, in a place deputed for them by His holy providence, and just where God would have them, it is not to be expressed what a sweetness they find in so loving a thought : and certainly they had infinitely rather be in Purgatory, to comply with His Divine pleasure, than be in Paradise, with violence to His justice, and a manifest breach of the ordinary laws of the house of God. I will say more, continued she : it cannot so much as steal into their thoughts to desire to be anywhere else than where they are. Seeing that God has so placed them, they are not at all troubled that others get out before them ; and they are so absorbed

in this profound meditation, of being at God's disposal, in the bosom of His sweet providence, that
they cannot so much as dream of being anywhere
else. So that, methinks, those kind expressions of
Almighty God by His prophets, to His chosen people,
may be fitly applied to the unhappy and yet happy
condition of these holy souls. Rejoice, My people,
says the living God ; for I swear unto you by Myself,
that when you shall pass through flames of fire, they
shall not hurt you : I shall be there with you ; I shall
take off the edge, and blunt the points, of those
piercing flames. I will raise the bright Aurora in your
darkness ; and the darkness of your nights shall out-
shine the mid-day. I will pour out My peace into
the midst of your hearts, and replenish your souls
with the bright shining lights of heaven. You shall
be as a paradise of delights, bedewed with a living
fountain of heavenly waters. You shall rejoice in
your Creator, and I will raise you above the height of
mountains, and nourish you with manna and the sweet
inheritance of Jacob ; for the mouth of the Lord
hath spoke it : and it cannot fail, but shall be sure
to fall out so, because He hath spoken it.

Did we truly know what is the pure love of God,
a love without interest, and a heart that neither has,
nor will have, any other ends, feelings or designs, but
those of Almighty God, haply we might be able to
conceive a good part of the paradise of the souls in
Purgatory. Those holy souls see so clearly, how
much it imports them to have no other concern or
interest but for God's cause, that without the least
regard to their own sufferings, they had infinitely

rather dwell in Purgatory, since God will have it so, than be surrounded with the sweets of Paradise, without God's good pleasure : nay, more, though they had not the least blemish to wipe out, and the only question were to comply with God's blessed will, who, for some reason best known to Himself, were pleased to treat them in this severe fashion. This pure love, without all self-interest, is more forcible than any other consideration. For, if St. Paul could wish himself accursed for his brethren, if Moses could have been content to be blotted out of the book of life for the sake of God's people, if others have offered themselves to remain in Purgatory till Doomsday, to have the assurance of their own salvation, or to suffer for the good of others; and all this, either out of a kind of self-love, or an excess of fraternal charity, and while they were yet entangled with the apprehensions of this wicked world ; what may not a soul do which is full of divine love, without any mixture of self-interest, so purely refined as not to desire anything but God, and the execution of His inscrutable designs ? And since all holy souls are of this temper in the other world, I am confident there is not any one soul that would quit Purgatory, where God has placed her ; nor any that would not most willingly exchange heaven for Purgatory, should she discover the least inclination of God's will that it should be so. The Saints are much perfecter than mortal men ; who, notwithstanding all the weakness of frail nature, could have the heart to cast themselves into burning flames, when they saw it made for God's greater glory, and

could there sing out His praises. So happy did
they account themselves to have the power of
serving God, without any other interest than that
of His glory; nay, with the ruin of their very lives,
and all other worldly concerns.   And when they
had done all this, they would break out into tears;
as the most eloquent, though silent, expression of a
favour they never took themselves to deserve.
Wherefore, since all the souls in Purgatory have not
only a perfect, but also an experimental, knowledge
of this pure love, and withal see such a world of
devout souls, who are still pouring themselves out
into such heroical acts of pure love, how much, think
you, does this encourage them to do their best in
this kind?   And can you think, after all this, that
God will suffer Himself to be outdone in courtesy or
charity, and not be still furnishing them with a fresh
supply of new lights and celestial comforts?   And
certainly the attractions of Almighty God are not
to be numbered amongst His least favours.   They
do so transport a soul, and so absolutely master her,
that she neither feels nor cares for all the torments
in the world which the body suffers, while she is
thus absorbed, and even lost, as it were, in Almighty
God.   They applied caustics to St. Thomas of Aquin
while he was rapt in his profound speculations of
divinity, and he seemed not to feel the least smart,
or at least took no notice of it : he was so ravished
and drowned in Almighty God.   They tell the same
of the seraphical St. Francis ; how, when he was once
gone out of himself with an ardent affection of the
love of Jesus Christ, they applied the button cautery,

and the good Saint felt it no more than if it had been
a button of glass or crystal.   Many other servants of
God, in their ecstatical raptures and lofty meditations
of the joys of heaven, have been pricked with needles,
wounded with lances, and persecuted with rude blows,
cold water, hot irons, and the like: and yet, for all
this, could not be drawn out of their sweet quiet and
repose, to give the least attention to these rough entertainments.   What shall we say now of those fair souls,
lately flown out of their bodies, who are so forcibly
carried away with the pure love of God and His
eternal glory; who see themselves so near it, and
so certain to enjoy it, and to be swallowed up in
the immense ocean of the Divinity?   "If only my
son may be one day Emperor of Rome," said the
ambitious Agrippina, "I shall most readily consent
to be, soon after, thrown headlong into the bottomless sea."   And do you think those souls, who are
most certain to reign for ever in the empyrean
heaven, can complain of the fire wherewith they are
tormented for a few hours, or years, which are but
so many moments compared with eternity?   St.
Catharine of Genoa assures us, that God does so
violently, and withal so sweetly, attract and draw
after Him these happy souls, that it is impossible
to find out words to express it, or any parallel to
this sweet and loving violence.

This pure love which the souls have for Almighty
God goes not without a perfect conformity to His
Divine will.   And this is the thing which of all
others metamorphoses Purgatory into Paradise.   To
have the same will with Almighty God, says holy

F

St. Bernard,* is to be like God ; but not to have the
power to have any other but God's is to be what
God is, that is, content and happy in whatever condition.   If God, for some special reason, would have
a soul to be a million of years in Purgatory, without
fault, and without hope of any further merit, neither
the extremity of the pains, nor the length of the
delay, would rob her of that perfect resignation to
God's holy will.

Can there be any doubt of this, when we find souls,
even in this miserable life, so courageous and so conformable to the Divine pleasure, as to offer themselves
to be buried in hell-fire, if only it might but add one
single grain of increase to God's glory ?   No ; this
dei-formity, or uniformity to the designs of God's
providence, is so excessive great in these devout
souls, so vigorous and so puissant, that it cannot be
expressed or conceived in this our gross ignorant
world.   The Ecclesiastical History † assures us that
many of the holy martyrs, whilst they were in flames
of fire, melting off their lives by drops, as I may so
say, were heard to profess with a smiling countenance
and an invincible heart, that they took themselves to
be at a nuptial feast, and to tread upon roses. So well
were they pleased that God was so pleased, and that
His blessed will was performed in them ; nay, more;
that nothing grieved them but the shortness of their
torments, and the fleeting condition of their petty
martyrdoms, as they would call them.   "Ah," would
they say, "were this to last to the world's end, how

* St. Bernard, *Epist. ad Fr. de Monte Dic.*
      † Euseb. Niceph. Baron.

happy were we, and how welcome were our flames!"
by the light whereof one might clearly read the
fidelity of their hearts, and their conformity to the
Heart of the great God of heaven.

This excessive conformity and fidelity of these holy
souls makes them willing to cooperate with the sweet
rigours of God's justice against their crimes.   He who
loves God purely for Himself, loves all that belongs
to make up His glory ; and since God shows Himself
as much God in the exercise of His justice as in the
sweet influences of His boundless mercy, a happy
soul cannot choose but take pleasure to cooperate
with God's justice in procuring His satisfaction, even
at the charge of her own sufferings; and would most
readily annihilate herself for the honour of her God.
" If our hour be come," said the valorous Judas
Machabeus, "and if God have so disposed of us,
let us die, my brethren, and let us die bravely ; it
must be as the heavens have decreed, and I will
have it so, though at the cost of a hundred thousand
lives."   And holy Job : " Is it not reason," said he,
"that we should as well receive what we call evils
at the hand of His justice, as favours at the hand
of His mercy?"   That noble Roman that buried his
poniard in his own sister's breast, whom he met
foolishly bewailing the good fortune of the city of
Rome, had nothing to allege for his justification but
this—"What," said he, "shall not Rome be Rome,
as well in the exercise of rigorous justice as in the
maintenance of her greatness and demonstration of
her absolute power?   Can I offer a more pleasing
holocaust unto the gods than to sacrifice my sister,

F 2

when Rome's justice requires it?" This Roman
severity carries with it I know not what masculine
generosity; and this cruelty to a foolish sister argues
much piety to his dear country. And so, the holy
souls, that burn with ardent charity, seeing it necessary
that the Divine justice should receive plenary satisfaction, and that God's interest is extraordinarily concerned that His justice should rule by course, as well
as His mercy, goodness, and charity; these holy
souls, I say, seeing all this, have such a pleasure
in their torments as cannot be comprehended in
this miserable life, which is so full of self-love;
except by some few noble and generous souls, that
love God only for Himself, and that so purely,
as not to make any reckoning of their own concerns or sufferings.

§ 4.—*Another comfortable consideration, drawn
from the desire they have to make themselves
worthy of the sight of God.*

Take another consideration, which will much illus-
trate that which has been already said, and reinforce
the joy of the souls, in spite of their tormenting pains.
You may believe that a soul, having once taken leave
of the body, has such a passionate inclination to enjoy
her end, that is, to see God and to be united with
God, and finally to arrive unto that happiness, for
which she clearly sees she was created, that it can
hardly be expressed. A bird newly stolen out of the
cage wherein she was detained captive, flies not away
swifter; the furious course of a torrent, that pre-

cipitates itself from the top of a mountain, rolls not along with a greater impetuosity; the enraged winds, broke loose out of their close caverns underground, blow not with more violence, than the desire of seeing God thrusts on a soul once freed from the thraldom of the body.

Now, as they see in Purgatory that there is no other obstacle but the rust and filth of sin, and the remainder of their former misdemeanours, and that Purgatory fire is deputed by Almighty God to purify and refine them, and so to make them worthy of His presence, they are so far from grumbling or repining at this sweet rigour of God's justice, that, on the contrary, they take it for a greater favour and an extraordinary piece of mercy of Almighty God, their most loving Father. When they sawed off the leg of that great philosopher, he held it out with both his hands, he encouraged the operator, and perhaps also took hold of the saw himself, to do the surgeon that piece of service, saying, withal : "Let us thrust, my friend, let us thrust, and let us not fear to cut off this rotten and useless bone : the pain you give me will procure me a great deal of good, and the sooner we have done, the better. Be not afraid, then, my dear enemy ; but strike in thy saw boldly : the crueller thou art for the time, the sooner thou wilt put me out of pain." And thus the surgeon cut off his leg with as little sense or feeling as if it had been the leg of a statue, or of a person that had no relation to him, or was his mortal enemy. And that Japonian virgin,* who was to die by fire, could not

* Hist. Japan.

refrain from kissing the burning coals, and crying out
joyfully: "O lovely coals, O delicious flames, how
much am I obliged to your sweet cruelty, since you
put me in a condition of enjoying, within a few
moments, the only Spouse of my soul!" Oh, the souls
in Purgatory say the same with a far greater ardour
of love. And I venture to say more yet; that they
have such a longing desire to cooperate with God
in their own purification, and to render themselves
capable of the beatifical vision, that, if it were in
their power to heighten the rigour of their torments,
it would be the first thing they would do, to advance
their eternal felicity. And with reason; for if we
were, says St. Austin,* to take the pains of hell in
our way to see God in His glory, we ought to suffer
them with a good heart, for a good so great, that
whatsoever it costs, it can never be too dear. Think
well on these words, good reader: "Let God cost
never so much, He cannot be too dear."

St. Catharine of Genoa was heard to say, she
believed that the greatest pain which the souls have
in Purgatory, is to see they have an obstacle within
themselves, and some few blemishes, which hinder
them for the time from enjoying the sight of their
Creator; insomuch that their spite and anger is not
so much against the flames, though never so biting,
as against these unhappy blemishes and loathsome
remainder of their sins. Nay, they are, in a manner,
in love with the fire, which by little and little helps to
free them from this cruel pain; and they do like
the patient who kisses the razor that is to cut out

* Serm. 2. in Fest. Omn. Sanct.

whole slices of putrified flesh from a gangrene or
mortal ulcer, which would otherwise insensibly
bereave him of his life if that fierce remedy were
not applied.

§ 5.—*Their suffering without merit, and the free
exercise of their virtues without impediment,
are to them special motives of comfort.*

What a pleasure, think you, is it to suffer, or indeed
to exercise any virtuous act, merely for the virtue itself, without casting about for any further recompense
than barely the doing what is pleasing to Him we
love, and who loves us out of His pure bounty, without any desert of ours ! A Roman lady, understanding
that Cæsar had condemned her dear husband Pætus
to stab himself, snatched up the dagger first herself,
and struck it deep into her breast ; and then, with
a smiling but dying look, spoke thus to him : My
dearest, this stab has done me no harm at all ;
upon my honour, it has not ; but alas ! the stab you
are going to give yourself, it is that which bereaves
me of my life : and with that, she gave up the ghost.
Those holy and loving souls, calling to mind how
Christ died for them, to pay the ransom of their sins,
without looking for any return by way of recompense,
out of His pure charity, and obedience to His Father,
they would most willingly sacrifice themselves for His
glory, in satisfaction of justice, and imitation of His
charity ; and they scarce feel their pains, when they
compare them with those of their dear Redeemer.
We can, indeed, scarce apprehend this joy ; we that

are so selfish as to relish nothing but earthly things; whose hearts are so wedded to our own interests, and so apprehensive of pain. Yet, have the patience to listen to the pathetical expressions of a man even during this life, who certainly was not without his heavenly relishes, but could make a shift to find out a Paradise, even in the Purgatory of the sufferings of a miserable life. You will soon discover, by his golden eloquence, who it is that speaks. "Had I the choice to be an Apostle, Prophet, Doctor, nay more, an Angel and potentate of heaven; were it in my power to be metamorphosed into one of the Cherubim or Seraphim, and to be raised above their thrones; in a word, to be seated at the right hand of God; or else to be thrown down into a dark loathsome and subterraneous dungeon, there to be manacled, fettered, and grievously tormented, for the sole love of my Saviour Jesus Christ, in company with the glorious Apostle St. Paul: without all hesitation or doubt I should choose to be there with St. Paul, and should perfer it before the joys of heaven."* How do you feel your hearts, when you hear this kind of language? And what think you? may not the souls in Purgatory have the like affections, and more heroical, if there can be anything thought of more heroical than to quit heaven for Purgatory, and to leave God for God; sacrificing themselves entirely to His glory, as a perfect holocaust, to please His Divine will, and appease the sweet rigours of His justice?

Blessed Father Francis Borgia was wont to say, he would willingly go to Purgatory, and lie frying there

---

* St. Chrysostom, Hom. 8, in c. 4. Ephes.

to the end of the world, to heap up a new treasure of grace and glory, and to become a greater Saint in heaven, and a more acceptable servant to His Divine Majesty. In earnest, this was an act of a noble heart and purified soul, aspiring to the highest pitch of perfection. The holy man took it for a most incomparable satisfaction to see himself every moment to go on increasing in virtue, and heaping up graces upon graces, and at the last to purchase so high a place in the kingdom of heaven as not to have cause to envy the highest Seraphim. And yet, methinks, if I may have leave to vent my own thoughts, there is something of a holy kind of self-interest in this point of perfection; holy, I say, but withal, interest. But why may we not believe that those holy captive souls fly higher, and offer themselves to God, to suffer there for one another, out of a divine kind of civility and generous act of fraternal charity? For in this world there have been mothers who have chosen rather to die themselves then see their dear children die before them. There have been also souls, as I have touched elsewhere, who have wished to be damned (always understanding that it were without sin), to save others; and this without hope of grace, or glory, merely in obedience to perfect charity. And why should we make such a wonder of it, since the very tigress, who has no heart but what is made up of cruelty, has nevertheless love enough to cast herself into flames, if she find no other expedient to save her young ones? Can we believe that brutes have more love, and mortal men more charity and courage, then the holy souls of Purgatory have for the

love of God, and of those souls they passionately
love? O sweet Purgatory, O loving flames of charity,
and pure transcendent charity, worthy of the souls
which are so pure! The holy servant of God meant
this, when she said, that the souls are ·wholly
despoiled of all self-interest, and do wholly devote
themselves to God's interest; and that out of pure
charity.

We should soon see wonders in ourselves, would
we but give way to our virtues, and those divine graces
which are hourly showered down upon our souls from
heaven, to work according to the full extent of their
energy and power. But, alas! an infirm body, much
passion, a faint heart, with a thousand other obstacles
in this life, make us to do scarce half what we are able.
And divines are of opinion that, beside the Mother
of God, there hath hardly been one, amongst all other
pure creatures, who has acted according to the full
latitude of his power, and those gracious helps sent
him from heaven. Others, indeed, have sometimes
made valiant attempts; but it was, as it were, but in a
bravado and by spurts, and they often came off but
poorly, and failed in their designs. But the souls
in Purgatory, who are as it were new minted, and cast
into a pure spiritual substance, free from the body,
and all corporal and human infirmities, nor are at all
impeded by their torments from the free exercise of
all the powers of their souls; they, I say, give full
scope and liberty to all the choirs of virtues to play
their parts, and suffer grace to have her entire effect;
and this doubtless affords them such unspeakable
comforts and advantages, as cannot well be expressed

in this mortal-life. Oh, what ejaculations of their pure
love ! what submissions of their profound humility !
what conformities of their wills ! what submissive
obedience to the holy decrees of God's justice ! what
fidelity and justice, to satisfy the rigour of God's
justice for all they owe Him ! what passionate desire
of purity, to see themselves without blemish or
hindrance from enjoying God ! what incredible tenderness towards God, who treats them so sweetly in
comparison of their ingratitude and infidelity ! what
excess of joy to see themselves within two fingers'
breadth, as it were, of Paradise ! In fine, what a
paradise of virtues, what divine endeavours of these
happy souls ! what attractions of Almighty God, and
heavenly allurements ! Who can worthily comprehend
such a medley of so sweet a paradise in Purgatory,
so cruelly sweet and so lovingly bitter ? And now I
understand why St. Catharine said, that in case the
souls did not meet with Purgatory, it would be a kind
of hell to them, to want the help of those purging
flames to cancel out the blemishes of their sins, and
make them worthy to see God. I have not told you
what ejaculatory prayers they make, what sweet aspirations they breath out, and what flaming darts of love
they shoot up into the Heart of God. For if the
martyrs, in the greatest extremity of their torments,
could cast out such gentle sighs, and break into such
divine and loving speeches as to draw tears from the
eyes of a hangman or tyrant, what will not these holy
souls do, since they have scarce any sweeter entertainment then to converse with God and implore His
mercy ? The afflictions and sufferings of the body,

says Salvian,* cannot hinder the paradise of the soul
and her interior sweetness; much less, when the soul is
in the other world.

§ 6.—*They joy in the continual decrease of their pains, and influence of pure heavenly consolations.*

The fire of love works more sensibly with them than
their tormenting flames.   The natural instinct they
have to be with God, and their longing thirst to take
their fill of those inebriating joys, while they see
themselves forcibly detained and bound fast to so
base an element of fire, is a torment beyond expression.
St. Ambrose † maintains that the fire of love, which
had seized on St. Laurence's heart was more active
than that which consumed his flesh and melted the
very marrow of his bones.   Wherefore it must needs
be great comfort unto these sweet souls to see that
their sufferings are every moment diminished; if not
otherwise, at least forasmuch as concerns the prefixed
time of their durance, which goes lessening itself more
and more as it draws nearer to an end.   And, according to the probable opinion of holy men, the intensity
of the pain itself is perpetually decreased, according
to the fresh supplies of succour which the Church
militant never fails to administer unto them, by her
prayers and Sacrifices : since there is not an hour,
neither day nor night, when there is not Mass said or
some devout prayers offered up, in some part of the
Christian world.   Besides, St. Catharine tells us that

* *Lib. de Provid.*   † St. Ambrose, *Serm.* i.

God also grows still more and more liberal, in showering down His heavenly sweet favours and gracious
influences upon these wretched and yet happy souls.
There was a young woman, had lived with her
husband with so much chaste love, that she was not
more tender of her own life : and, seeing him one day
laid dead upon a burning pile, and having a long time
in vain cast about how she might come to him, at
length threw herself just upon his heart, and so chose
willingly to die with him, and mingle her ashes with
his. And who doubts but that the Guardian Angels,
those eagles of Paradise, seeing the souls of their
pupils, for whom they had so much tenderness and
care in this life, to lie burning in scorching flames,
often cast themselves in to comfort them; and, if not
release them, at least entertain them with such pleasing
discourses as take off much of the sense of their bitter
torments? When the King asked Daniel whether the
lions had not devoured him, and whether his God had
power to preserve him from that inevitable death, he
answered: Yes, Sir; my God has sent His Angel,
who is come down from heaven to protect me, and
has tied up the mouths of the hungry lions, who have
not offered to touch me: nor had I ever so much
comfort in my whole life, as in this place of death and
despair; for Paradise is everywhere, where God and
His Angels are. The same happened to those three
innocent young men, who had leisure to sing in the
middle of a burning furnace; which, from being a kind
of Purgatory was become a terrestrial Paradise, or an
empyrean heaven. This being so, and the goodness of
God comforting the souls with a world of good

thoughts, you must know that Purgatory seems a great mercy to them; and so much the greater, by how much they see clearly the vast difference between this condition of theirs and that of the damned souls; and what an unspeakable favour God has done them, to dispose things so sweetly, that they might be conveyed into Purgatory, they that so often deserved to be thrust into hell-fire; and possibly more than many of the damned souls: since there are certainly many damned but for one or two mortal sins, whereas they may know themselves to have committed thousands. And who knows, then, whether in their ecstasies of love they may not cry out, with holy St. Gregory: "O my God, increase my griefs; alas! I have deserved far more; but withal be pleased, I beseech Thee, to remember in Thy mercy to increase also my courage, and to fortify my patience."

Nothing, surely, is comparable to pure heavenly consolations. When all creatures are wanting, and all other worldly satisfactions eclipsed from our hearts, so that we remain in pure sufferance, and taste nothing but God alone, then it is, say the mystical divines, that we possess the joy of all joys, and the quintessence of all true and solid comfort. "God has done us the honour," says St. Paul, "to make us sit by His Divine Majesty, and, as it were, side by side to His Son Jesus Christ;" a favour that has so ravished my soul, that I cannot think on it without incredible joy. "Where, do you imagine, was St. Paul," says St. Chrysostom, "when he spoke this? For my part, I believe he was lying in a dungeon, in irons, neck and heels together, forsaken of all the world; and that

it was in this general abandonment that he was surprised with those ravishing joys of heaven, and had
such a feeling of God's greatness, that he seemed to
be already seated at His right hand." "When, think
you," says St. Thomas, "was he rapt up into the
third heaven? I am apt to believe that it was at his
conversion, when, despoiled of all worldly comforts,
and all things failing him at once, Almighty God
snatched up his soul into heaven, and gave him a
sweet relish of the delights of Paradise." What shall I
say then of the souls, who, seeing themselves besieged
with fire and torments, and a thousand martyrdoms,
and having no human consolation, are put upon a
sweet necessity to have their recourse unto God, and
to seek their contentment in Him alone? Oh, what
fervent aspirations, what holy ecstasies, what cordial
oblations, what divine acts of conformity! How
lovingly doth God and His Angels inspire them! what
pure lights and affections do they instil l Hear the
Prophet David: "According to the multitude of my
bitter griefs, your consolations, O my God, have
rejoiced my heart." And St. Paul: "When I am
oppressed with evils, then it is that my soul swims in
celestial joys, and that I am as it were all candied with
sweetness." And the Prophet Isaias: "In the greatest
of your furies, in the severest rigour of your anger,
O my Lord, you have cast out some rays of your
sweet mercies, and have ravished me with admiration."
Now, though all this be said of this mortal life, yet
may we in some proportion give a guess by it, how it
fares with the holy souls in Purgatory; and the rather,
because a soul once severed from the body, has much

more liberty to produce its acts, and to couple an excess of torments with an excess of joys : since the same, in some sort, has been seen to have happened in this life. Have you ever read in St. Austin, that if a drop of the heavenly torrent should fall into hell, hell would no longer seem to be hell, but a kind of heaven? Now, certainly, the Divine Goodness lets fall some of those drops into Purgatory; nor are the Angels sparing, but rather prodigal, in showering them down upon souls who are to be exalted into heaven, as high as themselves, and possibly more.

But let not this discourse cool your charity; lest, seeing the souls enjoy so much comfort in Purgatory, your compassion for them grow slack, and so continue not equal to their desert. Remember, then, that notwithstanding all these comforts here rehearsed, the poor creatures cease not to be grievously tormented ; and consequently have extreme need of all your favourable assistance and pious endeavours. When Christ Jesus was in His bitter Agony, sweating blood and water, the superior part of His Soul enjoyed God and His glory, and yet His body was so oppressed with sorrow, that He was ready to die, and was content to be comforted by an Angel. In like manner, these holy souls have indeed great joys ; but feel withal such bitter torments, that they stand in great need of our help. So that you will much wrong them, and me too, to stand musing so long upon their joys, as not to afford them succour. Let us then here break off this discourse ; and pass on to consider what assistance we owe, and they expect of our charity ; and first, let us see what a charity it is to help them.

THE THIRD SURVEY.

THAT THERE IS NOT IN THIS WORLD A MORE EMINENT OR PRUDENT ACT OF FRATERNAL CHARITY, THAN TO HELP THE SOULS IN PURGATORY.

THE divine Apostle, the very disciple of Paradise, and doctor of the universe, reads us this lesson; that the highest point of Christian perfection consists in charity. The abridgment of the decalogue, the epitome of the whole Bible, the quintessence of all virtues, is finally reduced to this sole point of divine love. Now, fraternal charity, or the love of our neighbour, is cousin-german to the love of God; and upon these two holy loves, as upon the two poles of the world, moves the heaven of all perfections. They are the two angels that keep sentinel at the gates of Paradise;* the two Cherubim that cover the ark, where the manna of the felicity of this life is contained.† They are the two eyes of the spouse of the soul, which wound, as it were, the Heart of God, and pierce it so deeply with their divine glances, that He cries out in the Canticles,‡ that they have stolen away His Heart. "Alas," says He, "Thou hast wounded My Heart, My beloved, and hast robbed Me of it;" so powerful are the beauteous charms of this heavenly charity.

The more power the love of God has in us, the greater is the ardour of fraternal charity, which burns the very heart of our' souls, and, like the phœnix, takes

---

* Gen. iii. 24.   † 3 Kings viii. 7.   ‡ Cant. iv. 9.

G

delight to live and die in so noble a fire, and to consume in such health-giving and yet murderous flames.

My design here is, not to treat of the love of God,
but only to suppose that the more one loves God, the
more he loves and desires to help his neighbour: and
to believe that a man loves God without doing his
uttermost to assist his neighbour in the way of charity,
is to fool himself point-blank.   Would you know how
much you love God?   Look with what courage you
are wont to serve your neighbour; for otherwise, your
charity is not fire but smoke, and your affections are
not divine love, but empty air, or a mere natural love;
or, in a word, self-love, or rather, an empty shadow,
or fantastical appearance of divine love.   He that
loveth not his neighbour, whom he daily sees with
both his eyes, says St. John,* how can he make us
believe that he loves God, whom he never saw?

What I maintain is, that amongst all the acts of
fraternal charity or works of mercy, the most sublime,
the most pure, and the most advantageous of all others,
is the service we perform for the souls in Purgatory.

In the history of the incomparable Order of the
great St. Dominic, it is authentically related that one
of the first of those holy religious men was wont to
say, that he found himself not so much concerned to
pray for the souls in Purgatory, because they are
certain of their salvation; and that, upon this account,
we ought not, in his judgment, to be very solicitous
for them, but ought rather to bend our whole care to
help sinners, to convert the wicked, and to secure
such souls as are uncertain of their salvation, and

* 1 St. John iv. 20.

probably certain of their damnation, as leading very evil lives. Here it is, said he, it is here that **I** willingly employ my whole endeavours. It is upon these that I bestow my Masses and prayers, and all that little that is at my disposal; and thus I take it to be well bestowed. But upon souls that have an assurance of eternal happiness, and can never more lose God or offend Him, I believe not, said he, that one ought to be so solicitous. This certainly was but a poor and weak discourse, to give it no severer a censure; and the consequence of it was this, that the good man did not only himself forbear to help these poor souls, but, which was worse, dissuaded others from doing it; and, under colour of a greater charity, withdrew that succour which otherwise good people would liberally have afforded them. But God took their cause in hand; for, permitting the souls to appear and show themselves in frightful shapes, and to haunt the good man by night and day without respite, still filling his fancy with dreadful imaginations, and his eyes with terrible spectacles, and withal letting him know who they were, and why with God's permission they so importuned him with their troublesome visits, you may believe the good Father became so affectionately kind to the souls in Purgatory, bestowed so many Masses and prayers upon them, preached so fervently in their behalf, stirred up so many to the same devotion, that it is a thing incredible to believe, and not to be expressed with eloquence. Never did you see so many and so clear and convincing reasons as he alleged, to demonstrate that it is the most eminent piece of fraternal charity in this life to pray for the souls departed. Love and fear are the two most excellent orators in the world: they can teach all rhetoric in a moment, and infuse a most miraculous eloquence. This good Father, who thought he should have been frightened to death, was grown so fearful of a second assault, that he bent his whole understanding to invent the most pressing and convincing arguments to stir up the world both to pity and to piety, and so persuade souls to help souls: and it is incredible what good ensued thereupon. The history does not set down the motives which he either invented, or had by inspiration, to evidence this truth; and therefore I will borrow them of St. Thomas, that angel of divinity, of the same Order, and of other Saints and Doctors of the Catholic Church.

§ 1.—*The greatness of the charity to the souls in Purgatory is argued from the greatness of their pains and their helpless condition.*

Since there is no torment under heaven comparable to the pains of Purgatory, as we have already seen, those unhappy souls must needs be the most afflicted creatures in the world; and consequently there cannot be a greater charity than to relieve them. The loving mother runs always to her sickliest child: not but that she is tender of them all, and has her heart divided into as many parcels as she has children, and sick children; but where there is most need, there she makes a greater demonstration of her love; thither her heart is carried with a greater violence and ten-

derness of affection, where the greatest evil or danger
appears. As for the rest, their condition is not so
pressing; she speaks to them at leisure, and by giving
one of them a few comfits, a good word to another, a
smile to a third, they are all well contented. But he
that burns in the Purgatory of a violent fever, it is he
that hath most need of his mother: and so you see
her, as it were, nailed to his pillow, her heart, her
eyes, her hands, her mouth, and her very bosom lie
open to this child, and she can think of nothing but
him: so that, where there is a greater share of misery,
reason requires there should be more compassion and
more charity expressed. Cast but a morsel of bread
to a needy beggar; send a good alms to a needy
hospital; visit a prisoner; give a word of comfort to a
sick person; and they are very well satisfied. But he
that lies burning in unmerciful flames, ah, it is he that
ought to move all the bowels of your compassion.
When the image of Cleopatra, with the stinging asps
at her breasts, was carried in triumph before the
Romans; though otherwise fierce and cruel enough by
nature, yet could they not hold from shedding a few
tears of compassion. The other captives, yet living,
did not move them at all, in comparison of that unfortunate princess, though she was only represented in
colours upon a painted cloth. You angel-keepers of
Purgatory, I conjure you to unlock your gates and lay
your prison open, that I may discover those kings and
queens, I mean those holy souls of both sexes, who
are shortly to have their share in the heavenly kingdom; that I may lay before the eyes of the whole
Catholic Church those asps of grief, that lie so close

at their breasts; those cruel flames, I mean, that incessantly devour them, and at the same time the infinite modesty and patience with which they endure
all; insomuch that not one of them lets fall the least
froward or inconsiderate word, or makes the least
complaint against the sweet rigour of God.   Is there
a heart, if it be the heart of a man indeed, and has
but a drop of true Christian blood in it, that does not
feel itself to be either broken or softened at so lamentable a spectacle; to see, I say, such noble and
generous spirits in so deplorable a condition?   Is
there anything within the whole circumference of the
universe so worthy of compassion, and that may so
deservedly claim the greatest share in all your devotions and charities, as to see our fathers, our mothers,
our nearest and dearest relations, to lie broiling in
cruel flames, and to cry to us for help with tears that
are able to move cruelty itself?   Whence I conclude,
there is not upon the earth any object that deserves
more commiseration than this, nor where fraternal
charity can better employ all her forces.

Next to the grievousness of their pains, there is not
anything can so enlarge your charity to deceased souls,
as the nature of their condition, wherein they can
neither help themselves nor one another.   For there
is no more time for merit: alas, no; nor any way
left them to solace themselves in the least degree, but
merely to suffer patiently the sweet rigours of the
Divine justice.   Here upon earth, there is not a
creature so wretched but can both help himself, and
receive help of others.   At least, he has his comfort,
that he merits heaven by his sufferings, and that his

patience will prepare him a crown of glory. He may exercise a thousand acts of virtue, which are as many degrees of grace and glory, if he do them as he ought. He makes a virtue of necessity, by embracing that voluntarily which he cannot avoid; and glories in this, that he can imitate his Saviour Jesus Christ. Whereas, the souls can receive no comfort by meriting, which is the comfort of comforts in this life: whence I conclude, that our charity to them cannot be better employed.

When our Blessed Saviour saw that poor creature, and heard him say, that he had lain there perishing at the pond side for the space of thirty-eight years, for want of a man to help him in, it went to the very Heart of sweet Jesus; and, presently forsaking all others, He cured this poor impotent creature, and wrought that famous miracle in favour of this helpless wretch, forsaken of the whole world besides. And certainly, this was a case of great commiseration; but nothing comparable to the case we treat of. For those that are yet living, though never so miserable, have a thousand tricks and devices to shift and help themselves in their miseries; but the poor souls, alas! have no way left them, to decline or sweeten their martyrdom. Pliny reports that an eagle, seeing, one day, the young maid his dear mistress, who had cherished him in her bosom, laid on a burning wood pile, was so struck at the sight, what with love and what with compassion, that he immediately took wing and launched into the burning flames to deliver her. Good God! shall savage beasts, and that tyrant of the air, have more pity of a dead carcass, that feels

nothing, than we have of immortal souls, who have
so great a feeling of insupportable torments? Your
Indian women use to hold it for a great honour, to
throw themselves into the flames to their dead
husbands, and so to join souls and ashes together.
And shall it be said that a natural love is more daring
than a supernatural; and that these Indian women
have more love for the dead carcasses of their husbands, than we have for the precious souls of our
fathers, mothers, brothers, sisters, and others, who are
most worthy of incomparable love?

§ 2.—*Our charity for the souls departed is preferred before all other works of mercy.*

You shall be judge yourself, you that read this.
If God at the same instant, should put you both in
Purgatory and in a common gaol, as it is most easy
for Him to do; I conjure you to tell me, in which
of the two places would you desire to be first relieved? And ought you not to do that for others
which you would have them to do for you?

Besides, the spiritual works of mercy are of a higher
rank than those that are corporal; as St. Thomas
proves excellently well. Is it not, then, a more noble
piece of charity to relieve souls than bodies; to stretch
out your hand, I say, to help a poor soul out of
scorching flames, than to comfort a sick person, that
feels but a little heat of a fever, and may have a
thousand sweets and refreshments?

Again; when you bestow an alms on a poor body,
tis true, you can never do amiss, if you look only on

God; but you may often fail of your aim, and lose
both your money and your labour, if you consider the
men themselves ; who for the most part are ungrateful, deceitful, wicked, and so far unsatisfied, that
you have never done with them. Do them a thousand
good turns; if you fail but once, all is lost; they do
nothing but grumble and repine : they quite forget all
the good they have so plentifully received from your
accustomed liberality; they take notice of nothing but
what you have omitted. They believe all is no more
than their due ; they are as insolent as if you were
always bound to do for them. To say nothing, that
they often abuse your charity, and serve themselves of
your gracious benevolences to offend both God and
man ; as being notorious gluttons, drunkards, blasphe-
mers, and abominable villains, both for body and
soul.

But the good you do for souls, so beautiful, so
noble, and so holy, besides the reward you shall be
sure to receive from God, it is not to be imagined
how well it is bestowed, and how grateful they are for
it. There is nothing lost, though you give ever so
little : they take themselves to be infinitely obliged
for your charity; they never forget it; they never
complain; they never turn ungrateful. Certainly, it
must needs be an unspeakable advantage to you, to
be assured that the good you do is for a happy soul,
though unhappy for the time ; for a Saint that is ready
to be canonized in heaven; and, perchance, after a
few more moments of pain, shall be a greater Saint
there, than many whose feasts we keep with great
solemnity ! Besides, it cannot but be an excessive

comfort to oblige a soul which loves God with all
its strength, and which will soon lodge in His very
Heart. Lastly, (what an honour must it be, thus to
contribute to the glory of so happy a soul, who within
a while shall be brighter than the sun, and a com-
panion to the Angels, and shall exercise a world of
most sublime acts of virtue, of thanksgiving to God,
fraternal charity, and the like !) And if you chance
to go yourself into Purgatory, before they are released,
you will be exceedingly rejoiced to see what a grateful
remembrance they have of your charity, and would
not, for all the treasures in the world, but have done
that little you have done for them ; and you will
scarce have a more sensible feeling for anything, than
for having lost so many occasions of relieving so many
poor souls in their grievous torments.

Our Blessed Saviour tells us, whosoever bestows a
charity on a disciple, or on a prophet, shall be sure to
have the reward of a disciple or of a prophet. Now,
as long as your charity extends itself only to the living,
let your motive be never so pure, and for the love of
God, alas, you are often deceived, and think you do
a good turn for an Apostle, and he is an apostate, or
another Judas. You take him for a great servant of
God ; and he often proves to be a most wicked fellow :
a ravenous wolf in a lamb's skin. And this is seen
daily, and everywhere : not but that you ought to do
it, and shall never want your reward. But it falls out
clear otherwise, when you place your charity upon the
souls in Purgatory ; for they are undoubtedly the
disciples of Christ ; they are prophets and great
Saints ; and therefore, whosoever shall do any charit-

able office for them, may well hope to have the reward of Saints. For so, it is not only those that are thus relieved shall be translated into heaven, but those also that relieve them shall be carried thither in due time, to take possession of the glory of the Saints.

St. Thomas tells us, there is an order to be observed in our works of charity to our neighbour : that is, we are to see where there is a greater obligation, a greater necessity, a greater merit, and the like circumstances. Now, where is there more necessity, or more obligation, than to run to the fire, and to help those that lie there, and are not able to get out? Where can you have more merit, than to have a hand in raising up so great Saints and servants of God? Where have you more assurance, than where you are sure to lose nothing? Where can you find an object of more compassion, than where there is the greatest misery in the world? Where is there seen more of God's glory, than to send new Saints into heaven to praise God eternally? Lastly, where can you show more charity, and more of the love of God, than to employ your tears, your sighs, your goods, your hands, your heart, your life, and all your devotion, to procure a good that surpasses all other goods ; I mean, to make souls happy for all eternity, by translating them into heavenly joys, out of insupportable torments? That glorious Apostle of the Indies, St. Francis Xavier, could run from one end of the world to the other, to convert a soul, and think it no long journey. The dangers by sea and land seemed sweet, the tempests pleasing, the labour easy, and his whole time well

employed. Good God! What an advantage have
we, that with so little trouble and few prayers, may
send a thousand beautiful souls into heaven, without
the least hazard of losing anything? St. Xavier could
not be certain that the Japonians, for example, whom
he baptized, would persevere in their faith; and,
though they should persevere in it; he could have as
little certainty of their salvation. Now, it is an article
of our faith, that the holy souls in Purgatory are in
grace, and shall assuredly one day enter into the
kingdom of heaven.

But, since I am entered upon the point of seeking
God's greater glory, and procuring that His Sacred
Majesty be worthily adored by His creatures, where
can you find anything among all the other works of
mercy, more eminent in this kind than to concur
towards the peopling of Paradise, and increasing
the number of those thrice happy souls? Let it be
by never so little that you advance the term appointed
for the eternal happiness of a soul, by recovering it
out of Purgatory and placing it above the firmament;
oh, into what acts of love will she break forth? what
glory will she give to God? what excess of love, what
transports, visions, unions, and miracles of heaven,
will ensue? And what a happiness is it for you to
have concurred to make up all these wonders, which
would have been quite lost all this time, and by your
occasion are now added as a superabundant increase
of God's glory!

St. Ignatius, that glorious founder of the Society of
Jesus, hesitated not to say, he should think his whole
life well bestowed, should he but hinder an ungracious

soul from offending God one only night. Such an esteem he had of increasing God's glory, and such an apprehension of diminishing the least grain thereof. What a mercy is it, then, that by helping a soul out of its purging flames, you are the cause of a million of most divine acts, which would never have been, had not the time of its delivery been antedated by your charitable and devout prayers. Tell me, dear reader, what can you do here below, comparable to this? How many thousand beggars, prisoners, and sick persons may you relieve, without procuring the thousandth part of this unspeakable good? That which one does by another's means, he is accounted to do himself. So that all the new Saints, I mean, all the souls who have been delivered by your assistance, shall be, as it were, your lieutenants, and your vicar-generals, or your ambassadors, to do incomparable wonders in heaven, whereof you are the cause, in whole or in part. And what comparison is there, now, between the good we do for men upon earth; and what we do to relieve souls in the other world?

There is but one only case that can be imagined, in which your charity might seem clear better employed than in comforting the poor languishing souls in Purgatory. And it is this: suppose that you had but one instant of life at your disposal, and could either employ it in the conversion of a desperate sinner, who must otherwise be infallibly damned without redemption, or in relieving a soul in Purgatory: whether you ought not, in this case, to prefer the eternal salvation of a sinner before the present ease of a soul in Purgatory? To this I answer, that, in the first place, you put a very metaphysical case, far remote from all common practice; for it is not a thing that will probably ever happen. But, should it really fall out, then, in God's name, do the one or the other, as God shall inspire you: and God will sooner multiply the bread in your hands, than you should want an occasion of relieving the poor, whether living or dead. But to give you better satisfaction, put the case as you please, and I will make the souls in Purgatory themselves judges of the cause; that they may have no reason to complain, or appeal from my sentence.

They will certainly tell you, that where there is question of a mortal sin, or of the eternal loss of a soul that has been ransomed with the Blood of Christ, they had rather lie still groaning under their torments, than purchase a little ease at so dear a rate.

No, they are not so selfish; their love is more pure than so: their fidelity to God will never suffer them to seek their own glory, with the least diminution or lessening of God's glory. St. Catharine of Siena begged two years together, with tears in her eyes, that she might be damned for all mankind; and that she alone might suffer all the pains of hell, rather than any one soul should be damned, or her dearest Spouse grievously offended. And do you believe that a tender virgin, made of flesh and blood, and as yet a sinner, at least so far as to be guilty of certain venial transgressions, can have less self-love, more courage, and more of the love of God, than the souls of the other world, who are totally disengaged

from all self-respects, and love God only with a
most perfect love? No; they had rather double and
redouble their cruel martyrdoms, with a million of
fresh torments, than willingly give consent that, for
their sakes, one should forbear to hinder the commission of a mortal sin, or the damnation of a soul.
And, therefore, should the case fall in your way, stick
not to bestow your time for the benefit of the living:
do not so much as think on the souls in Purgatory,
who would most willingly melt themselves away in
tormenting fire, rather than permit such a horrible
mischief.

§ 3.—*Of the great advantages we receive by this
devotion for the souls departed.*

But, to come nearer to you, seeing that interest
rules the world most, and is the spirit that moves the
whole universe, if you are at all sensible of your own
interest, I mean a holy interest, allowed of by God
Himself, to wit, an interest which we all have in the
increase of our grace, glory, and eternal happiness;
in God's name, do all the good you can for your
neighbour. Except only the case I lately spoke of,
I defy you to do the thing that can bring you so
much true and solid good, or be of so much advantage to you, as is the striving to relieve the souls in
Purgatory.

And first; though it were true (as many will have it)
that the souls in Purgatory are not able to obtain the
least mercy of Almighty God, for themselves, or us, in
respect of their present confinement, in which they lie,

as it were, at pawn, and under a most severe restraint
and strict seizure, yet have we reason to believe their
good Angels will supply their defect, and not fail to
requite you for seconding them so well in delivering
the souls under their charge, for whom they are in a
kind of pain, to see them endure so much pain, and
yet to be held back, as it were, only by a small thread,
from enjoying their full liberty, and becoming their
companions, and as glorious as themselves.   One
sigh, or sob, one tear of yours, shed for these captive
souls, is enough to cut the thread, and then they will
cry out with holy David : Our souls are got loose, like
the innocent sparrow, and are flown up to heaven ;
having happily broken the iron nets that held them
bound to hellish fire.   The holy Name of God be ever
blessed, and they also who have been so kind as to
call upon Him in our behalfs.   It is you, dear reader,
to whom these holy souls address their speech, whom
you have comforted with a good wish, or with a tear,
or with a Mass, or with a Communion.

But suppose the Angels should neglect to perform
this good office, which notwithstanding we have reason
to expect of their charity; God Himself would not fail
to do it.   For, beholding the zeal with which you
burn, and the charity which impels you to succour
those tormented souls, whom He loves, and for
whom He has prepared eternal laurels and rich
crowns of immortal glory, can you doubt whether
He takes it well that you love these His dear
friends, that you have a tender heart towards those
He so tenderly loves, that you do this good work,
believing (as it is most true) that this is fraternal

charity in the highest point of its perfection, and that, making choice of it to serve God in the best manner by yourself, and by those holy souls, His infinite Goodness is highly pleased with your charity so well bestowed, and on so good a subject?

Mark well the reason I am now going about to lay down before you.   Christ Jesus has vouchsafed to honour His Church so far as to style it His Body, of which He is the Divine Head.   Now, it is most certain, that of all the members of this most sacred and mystical Body, that which is the most oppressed with evils, and the most lamentably afflicted, are these dear souls, who are, alas, most severely treated in the bosom of the Church suffering; since there is not any torment in the world that is comparable to theirs, as you have seen elsewhere.

If, then, our Blessed Saviour see your heart melt with compassion for that part of His Body which is the most comfortless and the most afflicted of all others, sure He must needs love you with a paternal affection, and give you a thousand benedictions for the ease and comfort you give Him in that part of His Body which suffers most.   Historians tell us, how a man having one day plucked out a thorn out of a lion's foot, the generous beast, feeling himself eased in that part which was most grieved, soon forgot his fierce nature, and by force of love and gratitude metamorphosed himself into a lamb, to wait upon this saviour of his, who had thus preserved his life; and, by way of requital, in a like occasion of danger, saved the man's life also, to the astonishment of all the beholders.   God plays the lion of Juda below in

H

Purgatory, permitting His justice to sway the sceptre of rigour. Now, if you but pull out the thorn out of His Foot, that is, if you ease Him in that part of His mystical Body which suffers the pains of Purgatory, this Lion will soon become a Lamb: He will not only save these poor souls, but when you yourself are in most need, as when you are struggling for life, He will show Himself, He will fight for you, and will give you the true life; in a word, He will make you clearly see how well He takes it, that you have plucked out the thorn out of His Foot.

Now, let us suppose the worst. Put the case, that neither God nor His Angels do requite you. Yet I maintain, you cannot do an act of fraternal charity wherein your gain is so great and so certain as this. I do not only say this, because the men of this world are commonly in an ill state, in which their prayers can do you no service. I do not only say it because, though you suppose them to be in a state of grace, yet is their devotion for you soon at an end, and, while it lasts, is but a slender, cold, and untoward piece of service.

I do not only say that these souls, who are truly miserable, and yet holy, under a cruel restraint, and yet happy, not able to merit anything, and yet gracious in the sight of His Divine Majesty:—I do not only say, that when they are once got into Paradise, they will be so many Guardian Angels of yours, so many advocates to plead your cause at the grand Tribunal of the most Holy Trinity, so many patrons and sureties for you and yours. But I say, that even while they remain prisoners, they will do miracles for you.

I said, miracles. Now hear how they will do that which cannot be done. They will effect that for you which they cannot do for themselves; and, were it necessary to work a miracle in good earnest, they would sooner do it than forsake you in your necessities. I am not ignorant that the Angelical Doctor* teaches, that those unhappy souls are in such a wretched state, that they have more need to beg our prayers than to pray for us; that they are wholly taken up with paying their debts to God's justice, who exacts an account of them to the last farthing; that this suffering Church is rather in a condition to suffer than to act anything; that it is not now a time to merit, but to burn; not to succour those that are living, but to expect succour from them. A man that is drowning has not leisure to think of others; a notorious malefactor, that swims in boiling oil, is not in a place where he ought, or can, plead for another; his whole mind is so plunged in the oil, and all his thoughts so overwhelmed with the boiling liquor that torments him. Alas! those racked souls have more reason to cry out, with holy Job: Ah, you my friends, you at least take pity of me, for the hand of God's justice, so lovingly severe, hangs continually over me, and strikes me without intermission; cease not to pour out your prayers for me, to abate the rigour of His justice with your charitable sighs, for a most miserable soul.† They have, I say, more need to beg our prayers than to pray for us. I know well, that many learned Doctors are of opinion, that the souls in Purgatory do not

* St. Thomas, 2, 2, 9, 83, a. 11, ad. 3.   † Job xix. 21.

H 2

pray for us.   But it is no point of our faith; and
therefore they must give me leave to side with other
great divines, who very probably maintain that those
grateful souls pray most ardently for those that pray
for them.*   The rich glutton, though he was certainly
damned, could pray, after his fashion, for his brothers :
and shall not a holy soul have the power to do it?
Abraham argued the case with him; called him,
lovingly, son;† and seemed to be upon the point
of doing something for him; at least, gave him the
comfort to tell him, that his brothers had Moses and
the prophets to instruct them : as if he would have
said, that if his brothers had not been sufficiently
provided of other means, he would peradventure have
granted him his request, and sent Lazarus to preach
to them.   But to give you a stronger‡ instance.   The
devils themselves have put up their requests to God,
and have been heard, and obtained that sorry comfort
they desired : as when they desired not to be thrust
down into hell, and got leave to enter into the herd
of swine, and then throw themselves into the sea.§
What! shall the damned souls pray, and shall the
devils be able to obtain their request, and shall not
the souls in Purgatory have the like privileges?
St. Thomas does not deny that they pray for us;
but only affirms that they have more need of our

* Bell. *De Purgatorio*, lib. 2, c. 17; Suarez, d. 47, sec. 2;
De Oratione, lib. i. c. 11.

† St. Luke xvi. 25.

‡ The original has "stranger," which perhaps is the true
reading.

§ St. Matt. viii. 31.

prayers; which is most true, but may well consist with their praying for us. A wicked felon, that is going to be turned off the ladder, has yet a care to pray for his whole family, for the King and the whole Bench, that condemned him, and many times for the very hangman too, who is ready to strangle him. And shall this wretch have more power, or more zeal, or more grace, than those souls, who are so holy, and who, in spite of their torments, are very present to themselves, and have their wits about them, free from all trouble and disquiet, which might rob them of the sentiment and feeling which they ought to have, of the obligation they owe to the charity of those that pray for them? Oh, no: they do the one, and yet neglect not the other. They pray for themselves in suffering, they pray for us in sighing; and the one hinders not the other in Purgatory, since even here upon earth, the soul that is immersed in flesh and blood can perform both parts; that is, satisfy for herself, and yet have a solicitous care of others. Did not Onias and Hieremias pray affectionately for the people of God whilst they were in the dark prison of Abraham's bosom? And do not the Saints assure us, that God wrought a miracle for the merits of St. Paschasius, who yet, nevertheless, was not out of Purgatory?* The same is reported of St. Severin; and though there be some dispute who this St. Severin was, yet the authors doubt not but that a Saint in Purgatory may work a miracle by God's permission. Some that are damned have wrought miracles; and is it such a wonder that

* St. Gregory, *Dialogue* 4.

we should allow this to the Saints of God's suffering Church?

We read in the life of St. Catharine of Bologna, whose body, flesh and bone, is yet entire, and sits to this hour in a chair exposed to the view of the world, though it be above sixty years since her death—we read, I say, in her life (which has the approbation of the Apostolic See), that she had not only a strange tenderness for the souls, but a singular devotion to them, and was wont to recommend herself to them in all her necessities. The reason she alleged for it was this : that she had learnt of Almighty God how she had frequently obtained far greater favours by their intercession than by other means. And the story adds this ; that it often happened that what she begged of God, at the intercession of the Saints in heaven, she could never obtain of Him, and yet as soon as she addressed herself to the souls in Purgatory she had her suit instantly granted. Can there be any question but there are souls in that purging fire, who are of a higher pitch of sanctity, and of far greater merit in the sight of God, than a thousand and a thousand Saints, who are already glorious in the Court of heaven?

Tell me, was not our dread sovereign, during his late banishment, more puissant and more mighty than his subjects, who lived still in their own country, at their ease, and perhaps in greater plenty? for we see him no sooner restored to his undoubted right, but he is every way as great a king as his predecessors, as richly attired, as much courted by foreign princes, and as gloriously attended at Whitehall ; whereas the rest of his nobility and gentry are but his creatures and most humble servants.

There are great souls, that for some slight misdemeanours are banished out of the kingdom of heaven, to which they are heirs apparent, as being the adopted sons of God by grace; nay, more, are locked up in that burning furnace which we call Purgatory: but they are scarce let loose when you may see them come out in triumph, and go soaring up above the heavens, so high, as to lose sight of them. And when they are once there, what will they not do for you? And what did not our gracious King, according to his power, to honour and gratify those that stuck close to him in his misfortune, or were so lucky as to have a great hand in restoring him? King David, at his death, recommending his good servants to his son Solomon, spoke thus withal: "My son, there is such a one, and such a one, have well deserved death for the crimes they have committed; but when I was generally deserted, and when others took the boldness upon them to throw stones at me, these men took pity on me and gave me succour in my greatest affliction; and therefore I charge thee, O my dear son, to be mindful of them, and to favour them, as thou lovest me." Have not holy souls as much charity as David? Is not the misfortune into which they are fallen of a more sensible nature than his? In what a lofty strain will they then represent unto God the good service you have done for them in their extreme necessity, when they find themselves once securely seated in those heavenly mansions! And what will not that boundless mercy be moved to grant, at the instance of so dear friends?

Shall I tell you, there are many worthy persons who think these following words of Jesus Christ may be very properly applied to the souls in Purgatory? Do good, saith He, and make yourselves friends at the charge of your purses; and be good stewards of Mammon, the false god of riches, that those whom you relieve may assist you at the hour of your death, and lead you into eternal tabernacles. Among the poor, none so secure of enjoying the delights of 'Paradise as the souls in Purgatory, who are all predestinate, and all holy. For the present, they are poor indeed, and helpless creatures; but if you contribute never so little to their ease, they will be sure to requite you in your necessities; if not before, at least when they are once possessed of the joys of heaven.

Cardinal Baronius, a man of credit beyond exception, relates* how a person of rare virtue found himself dangerously assaulted at the hour of his death; and that in this agony he saw the heavens open, and about eight thousand champions, all covered with white armour, descend, who fell instantly to encourage him, by giving him this assurance, that they were come to fight for him, and to disengage him from that doubtful combat. And when, with infinite comfort, and tears in his eyes, he besought them to do him the favour to let him know who they were, that had so highly obliged him: "We are," said they, "the souls whom you have saved and delivered out of Purgatory; and now, to requite the favour, we are come down

* *In Annal. Eccles.*

to convey you instantly into heaven." And with that, he died.

We read such another story of St. Gertrude ;* how she was troubled at her death to think what must become of her, since she had given away all the rich treasure of her satisfactions to redeem other poor souls, without reserving anything to herself: but that our Blessed Saviour gave her the comfort to know, that she was not only to have the like favour of being immediately conducted into heaven out of this world, by those innumerable souls whom she had sent thither before her by her fervent prayers, but was there also to receive a hundred-fold of eternal glory in reward of her charity. By which examples we may learn, that we cannot make better use of our devotion and charity than this way. But he that will fully satisfy himself that he can lose nothing, but gain excessively, though he should offer up all his satisfactory works for the souls in Purgatory, let him read over what Father Eusebius Nierembergicus, and Father James Monford, have excellently well written upon this subject.

* Dion. Carthus. apud P. Roam, *De Purg.* c. 20.

THE FOURTH SURVEY.

OF THE POWERFUL MEANS TO QUENCH THE FLAMES OF PURGATORY.

COULD the poor souls but help themselves, or abate the cruelty of their torments with all their devout aspirations, so pure and so holy, they would soon free themselves. But, alas, they cannot: and this is one of their greatest miseries, to see themselves in so desperate a condition as to be overwhelmed with raging fire, and not to have the power to get out, or to allay the fury of the flames, or to merit the least favour in this kind; not so much as *de congruo*, as the scholastics speak, or by a certain congruity, harmony, or fitness. The time of meriting expired with' their lives; what now remains is wholly appointed for suffering: and it is not the least of their vexations, to see how easily they might have prevented all these mischiefs in their lifetime, and that now there is no remedy, but by suffering to supply for that negligence, though they would never so gladly. Howsoever, I love those divines,* who are something more civil in this point than their fellows; and am easily persuaded by them, that although the souls cannot immediately contribute the least to their own ransom, or any way merit their own deliverance, yet they may be so happy as to work upon the goodness of their Angels, and by their means obtain some sweet refreshments at the

* Suarez, sec. 3, d. 19, post. St. Thomas.

merciful hand of God, wherewith to allay the bitterness of their torments. And, following their opinion
who teach that they pray for us, and procure us
heavenly favours, what inconsequence were it, to say
further, that they move our good Angels to inspire us
efficaciously, to intercede for them, and to assist them
with all the duties of Christian charity? it being a
thing to which the holy Angels are otherwise of
themselves so much inclined, without the solicitation
or importunity of others.

§ I.—*What succour they receive from the Angels and Saints in heaven?*

In the first place, you would be resolved whether
the Angels and Saints in heaven, and above all, the
Mother of Mercy, pray really for them; and if so, how
comes it to pass that they do not every hour, or indeed
every instant, make a general gaol delivery, and quite
empty Purgatory? For what power has not the Mother
of God? What cannot so many millions of Angels
and Saints do? what can they be denied, in so favourable a request, for persons of so high merit? I answer,
that they pray for them, and pray in good earnest;
and I say further, that they are not content with a
quarant hour,* now and then, as our custom is, in
occasions of pressing necessity, but they keep a perpetual and constant course of prayer in heaven, in
favour of these holy souls.

This I take to be the pious belief of the Catholic
Church, as delivered by the whole sacred torrent of

* *i.e.* Obtaining a *quarantaine*, or Indulgence of forty days.

Doctors.* Nor is there the least reason why they should not do it; being not only powerful, but full of charity: especially when they remember that the like charity was bestowed on many of themselves; that the necessity of the souls is extreme urgent; that they are all members of one body, that they do not only concur to the glorification of their dear brethren, but are themselves to receive an additional increase of accidental glory, for having advanced the delivery of those precious souls, who perhaps may be holier than some of their own blessed company. Besides, this is a charitable office, suits well with their happy state, and there appears not the least inconvenience in it in this world. And yet, if this be so, one would think they might soon turn all the souls loose, and empty Purgatory, so that it were impossible for any soul to make any long stay there. Hold; you must pardon me, and not flatter yourselves too much with this vain credulity. You are to know, that the Saints are not such strangers to the decrees of Divine justice, as to beg the souls' release without punishment; for that were the way to destroy all justice. No; they aecommodate themselves to the laws of heaven, and willingly submit to the most equitable resolves of God's justice; amongst which it stands irrevocably decreed, that this life should be the place for mercy, but that justice should bear the sway in Purgatory. Do not then wonder, that the Saints do not obtain so extravagant a favour. The souls themselves, who are the most nearly concerned in their own sufferings, would be ashamed to demand it. Is it not reason, that God

* *Vide* Suarez, d. 48, sec. 5.

should be God in all His attributes, and exercise His justice as well as His mercy? We must take heed how we employ, or rather abuse, His clemency, so as to break down the laws of His justice. Would you then know what the Saints do?

First; they pray God to inspire the living to offer up their satisfactory works for the dead, and to find out a thousand inventions to help them.

Secondly; they strive to shorten the time, by procuring that the intensity of their pains may supply for the length and extension thereof: wherein there is no wrong done to justice, but only an exchange made of a long pain into a shorter one, but more violent; and yet this is an extraordinary favour: for you cannot imagine what an incomparable treasure is one day in heaven advanced before the time prefixed.

Thirdly; many Saints have left behind them a great treasure of satisfactions above what was due for their sins; so many holy innocent hermits, so many chaste virgins, so many great Saints of all Orders in God's Church, who lead such austere lives. Now, is it not very likely that these good Saints may pray God to apply the superabundance of these their merits and satisfactions to the poor souls in Purgatory? and who knows, whether the infinite goodness of God may not accept it for good payment?

Fourthly; why may we not piously imagine, that even those Saints who have no such remainder of merits, pray those that have it, to bestow it as an alms to relieve the poor souls? Sure, they are so courteous as not to deny anything to one another; especially in a case of so great commiseration: and why should they hoard up these precious treasures which cannot avail them? or how can they bestow them more charitably?

Fifthly; what harm were it to say, that the Saints beseech our Blessed Lady, and even Christ Himself, who has an infinite treasure of satisfactions in store, to apply some of their precious merits this way? I know the severer divines will not have it, that the Saints have recourse in this to our Blessed Saviour, who has determined what, and how, He will have this applied, according to the ordinary course and fixed laws of His Divine justice. But there be other Doctors of a milder temper, who believe He may be drawn sometimes to waive the extremity of rigour, and to dispense with His own laws; so that by extraordinary privilege we may hope for this favour of sweet Jesus and His Saints. And if other Saints have so much charity for the poor souls, you will think it but reasonable that the fathers and mothers (the same is to be said of other near relations) who are in heaven, and know that the souls of their dear children are locked up in that fiery furnace, will use all their possible endeavour, as far as God will give them leave, to fetch them out. But what shall I say of those Saints who were lifted up into heaven before their time, by the extraordinary assistance of the living, whose turn now it is to be in Purgatory? is it not very credible they will now requite their courtesy, and with usury too? For example: there may be a soul in Purgatory that has helped above a thousand other souls out of that place of torments. Can it be imagined, but that that regiment of Saints will do all they can, and more if it were possible, to deliver this their deliverer, and to

place him in the Court of heaven, who had so great
a hand in their timely preferment?   But, because we
are mere strangers to the style of that Court, and
nothing acquainted with the constitutions of that
Divine Monarchy, let us conclude only thus : That
whatsoever the Saints can do for the comfort of these
languishing souls, we may be sure they do it, and do
it punctually, without neglecting the least moment;
and, where they cannot prevail without breaking the
just decrees of their Sovereign, there they willingly.
acquiesce, and with due submission adore the Divine
justice.   So much for the Saints.   Let us now speak
of the souls themselves, and see

§ 2.—*Whether they are capable of being relieved by one another's prayers.*

It may be justly questioned whether the souls,
though altogether incapable of helping themselves in
their extreme misery, may not at least be permitted to
help one another by their devout prayers.   For if they
have the privilege to pray for the Saints in heaven,
that God will be pleased to increase their glory; if
they can pray for the living, as I endeavoured to
evince in the last section ; nay, if a damned soul may
have liberty to pray for his friends, as it seems to be
clear in the case of the rich glutton ; why may they
not be so kind as to pray for one another?   " If the
flames of hell," said the devout Sales, that worthy
prelate of Geneva, " were not sullied with the smoke
of sin, were they but pure flames of holy love, oh,
what a pleasure were it to be swallowed up by such

flames, or to be thus condemned eternally to love
God !" What should hinder, then, but that the souls
in Purgatory, where the fire of love triumphs over
their tormenting flames, may display their ardent
charity, and vigorously apply themselves to assist and
comfort one another, as far as God's providence will
give them leave? May we not presume to fancy, that
out of an excess of charity they are willing to despoil
themselves of all those helps and advantages, which
they receive from their friends, to throw them upon
others, offering themselves freely to suffer for one
another? Tertullian* admires how prodigal the first
Christians were in this kind of charity; of suffering,
and even dying for one another; how ready they were
to leap into the very flames, and expose themselves to
the most cruel tortures that could be devised; and all
to save others, for whom they were prepared. What?
shall frail mortals, who are made up of flesh and
blood, thus willingly suffer for one another, and shall
not the souls, who have cast off, with their bodies, all
human weakness and imperfection, have as much
charity for other souls? Especially, being certain of
their salvation, of which men in this life can have no
assurance, without a particular revelation.

Didymus offered to die for St. Theodora; and finally
died both for her, and with her.† Eliseus, being dead
himself, raised another from death to life; which was
more than he did for himself. St. Paul would have
been content to be anathema, to save the Jews, always
under condition, that it might be without sin. David
would willingly have met with death in her ugliest.

* Tertullian, *Apolog.*   † St. Ambrose, *De Virgin.*

attire, so he might have saved his son Absalom; and yet he knew him to be but a graceless and unnatural parricide. Shall not holy souls have as much kindness for other souls, whom they see upon the point of being metamorphosed into Seraphim, as David had for a mere reprobate and lost creature? Many Saints in this world have begged it as a favour of Almighty God, that they might suffer for the souls in Purgatory; and have done it in good earnest, freely renouncing their own conveniences for the souls' comfort, by a most heroical act of supernatural charity. Do not you believe, that the souls in Purgatory have a more refined love, and that they actuate themselves in more heroical, transcendent acts of charity, since they are not only grown to be impeccable, but have withal a far clearer insight into the nature of this divine virtue? Aye, but—you say—they can merit nothing. True; but do you take them to be so selfish as to do nothing purely for God's sake, without seeking their own interest? What say you to our Guardian Angels? Is it for any private lucre or merit, or purely to please God, and to do us a work of singular charity, that they have so solicitous a care of us? And when God Himself loves us, is it, I pray you, for any interest of His own, or out of an excess of His overflowing bounty and charity, which well becomes Him? "Be perfect," saith He, "as I am perfect."* Now, the means to do this is, to be well versed in these acts of heroical love; as, to love God for God, because He deserves it, as being the only charming Object of our love. "I love," said St. Augustine, "because I love;

* St. Matt. v. 48.

I am resolved to love, because I am beloved of Him, that loves me only because He will needs love me." To love for mere love is the quintessence of divine love. What? shall we be so niggardly, so mercenary, or so mechanical, as not to exercise an act of pure love, without hope of reward? Is not our love well requited, if we please God, and those whom God loveth? They say, Apelles would give away his pictures for nothing; he had so great a value for them, he thought no set price could be equal to their worth, and that gold itself was too mean a thing to purchase such precious labours: which he therefore chose rather to give away gratis, than to expose to an unworthy sale. So that the bare pleasure he took in bestowing them upon his friends, was all the recompense he looked for, for those incomparable pieces. And certainly, it is a most noble and truly royal thing, to give, and to give without hope of requital.

Seneca spoke a word, which showed a magnanimous and true generous heart.* "To give, and to lose all benefit by one's gift, is no such wonderful thing; but to lose all benefit, and yet to be still giving, is a divine masterpiece, and an act worthy of God indeed." Now, when these charitable souls can gratify others, by giving away the charities which are bestowed on them, why should they not do it? To do a pleasure for another, without incommoding oneself, is no more than what you may expect of an Arabian, or barbarian; but to incommode oneself, to lie burning in fire, groaning under excessive torments; and all this to make others happy, is certainly an act worthy of those

* Seneca, *De Benef.*

CAN THEY PRAY ONE FOR ANOTHER?

noble and generous souls, who are all inflamed with
pure divine love. When the people had a mind to
flatter their Cæsars, they would cry out: "O Jupiter,
take away some of our years; shorten our lives,
decimate our days, and give it all to prolong the
life of our good prince! let him live, at the charge
of our lives: we are all ready to lay them down at
his feet, that he alone may live and reign happily,
in the flourishing greatness of his empire." Shall
infidels have more kindness for a mortal man, perhaps
a wicked tyrant, or a profane atheist, than holy souls
have for those that are about to be canonized as
Saints in the Church triumphant? I have heard of
great servants of God, who, when they saw some
famous preacher, or apostolical person, draw near to
his end, would express themselves to this purpose:
Oh, that I were permitted to die in his stead! for I,
alas, am but an unprofitable member of the Church;
all my services avail but little to advance God's cause:
whereas this worthy person may do a world of good,
and be a comfort to infinite souls. What should
hinder a soul in Purgatory from having the like
feeling? May she not, and with truth, cry out: I
am well acquainted with my own abilities, and can
have a near guess, what I am able to do in Paradise,
where I am like to be one of the meanest servants in
the whole house of God; and therefore may be well
spared. But there is such a soul: had she but once
cleared the petty debts she stands yet engaged for,
she would instantly mount above all the choirs of
Angels, and possibly soar up to the highest Seraphim.
Oh, that I might but have leave to suffer here awhile

in her place! how willingly would I do it, that so my
God might be the sooner and better glorified in
heaven by this happy soul, and a million of other
souls upon earth receive comfort and protection from
her powerful intercessions! I willingly resign unto
her all the right I have of being set free myself, and,
if God permit, I am ready to make her a deed of gift,
of all the suffrages which my dear friends have sent
me: for sure, all the pains which shall fall upon me
by this bargain, cannot but be lovingly sweet, since
they are the cause of so great a good in the imperial
Court of heaven. St. Christina was already lodged in
heaven, says Cardinal Bellarmine,* when she quitted
the glory of Paradise, to exchange it for the flames of
a thousand and a thousand most cruel martyrdoms.
And why may we not believe that souls so charitable
would willingly yet remain in their flames, that others
more worthy than themselves may be sent forth in
their stead, to glorify God in heaven? Whether God
accept of these holy desires or no, may be a question;
but at least it seems very credible, that the souls who
are so replenished with perfect charity, make such
tenders of their service, as far as God gives them leave,
and as far as it may stand with the laws of the Church
suffering. But enough of what passes in the other
world; of which we have no certain revelation, nor
other clear light to guide us by. Let us now turn our
speech to the living, and see what they are able to
perform for the benefit of the dead.

* _De gemitu col._ c. de Purg.

§ 3.—*That the dead may receive help from us that are living, and how we must be qualified, to do them good.*

Be pleased to take notice what several meanings these three words import; satisfaction, impetration, and suffrage. Satisfaction implies a good work, accompanied with some grief or pain, corresponding to the pleasure we unadvisedly took in sinning; whereby we make an honourable amends, and satisfy the laws of justice, by repairing the injury we have done. Impetration is a kind of letter of request, which we present to the mercy of God; beseeching Him to pardon those for whom we offer up the sacrifice of our devotions, and the incense of our sighs and prayers; so that our prayers address themselves solely to the mercy of God, and crave an absolute pardon, or abolishment of the crime, as a pure gift, without offering any proportionable satisfaction, save only that of our Blessed Saviour, or, in general, of the Church militant. Suffrage is a term which comprehends both; whether it be a penal work, or a prayer only, or both happily united together. The Church triumphant, to speak properly, cannot satisfy; because there is no place for penal works in the Court of heaven, whence all grief and pain are eternally banished.

Wherefore the Saints may well proceed by way of impetration and prayers; or, at most, represent their former satisfactions, which are carefully laid up in the treasury of the Church, in lieu of those which are

due from others : but as for any new satisfaction or
payment, derived from any penal act of their own,
it is not to be looked for in those happy mansions of
eternal glory.

The Church militant may do either ; as having this
advantage over the Church triumphant, that she can
help the souls in Purgatory by her prayers and satisfactory works, and by offering up her charitable
suffrages, wherewith to pay the debts of those poor
souls, who are run in arrear in point of satisfaction
due for their sins. Had they but fasted, prayed,
laboured, or suffered a little more in this life, they
had gone directly into heaven ; what they unhappily
neglected, we may supply for them ; and it will be
accepted for good payment, as from their bails and
sureties. You know, he that stands surety for another,
takes the whole debt upon himself; this is our case ;
for, the living as it were entering bond for the dead,
become responsible for their debts, and offer up fast
for fast, tears for tears, in the same measure and
proportion as they were liable to them ; and so defray
the debt of their friends at their own charge, and
make all clear.

This, then, is the general sense of the Church ;
that the living may help the afflicted souls in all these
several ways : either by satisfying for them, or by
their prayers, or by interposing the satisfactions of
Christ Jesus, who has left them at the disposition of
the Holy Church, His beloved Spouse. And what
rational person can deny this? since they are all
members of the same mystical body ; and consequently are bound in charity to yield mutual asssist-

ance and comfort to one another; and the rather, inasmuch as every one in his turn may stand in need of the same friendship, and look to be requited. " I am partaker,". said holy David, "with all those that fear Thee:"* and Holy Church to this purpose repeats that doleful ditty, so full of tenderness, out of Job · "Take pity on me, at least you that are my friends; for the hand of God has touched,"† yea, has fallen heavily upon me. And otherwise we must discredit a world of good authors, a world of authentical records, a world of most pregnant proofs, and blow upon the reputation of venerable antiquity, which has ever held it as one of the main points of Christian charity to pray fervently for the faithful departed, to pay their debts, and to strive, by all means possible, to help them out of their flames. To which purpose, by special favour, Almighty God has sometimes permitted souls to show themselves visibly to their friends and kindred,· to beg relief by Masses, prayers, and other good works, whereby to shorten and diminish the sharpness of their torments. So did Pope Innocent III., and a thousand others; as appears by unquestionable relations of grave authors. What they cannot do of themselves, they beg of us; and beg it as an alms for charity's sake : and it were both sin and shame to deny them. That which often costs us but little, they esteem at a high rate; and, could they but give us a clear sight of the wonderful effects of our small endeavours, we should questionless take their cause more to heart than we do. However, St. Thomas and other divines

* Psalm cxviii. 63.   † Job xix. 21.

assure us that, even in rigour of justice, our satisfactions are accepted in lieu of theirs; since God has so ordained and passed His word for it to His dear Spouse the Church, who really believes it to be so, and proceeds accordingly. So that we may rest confident, that whosoever undertakes to provide for those distressed souls, so he be qualified with the conditions which are requisite on his part, shall infallibly relieve them. Well; but you long now to know what these conditions are, with which we may be most certain that our suffrages are effectual towards the purifying and releasing of the poor souls in Purgatory.

He that will have his works acceptable in the sight of God, for the obtaining of any mercy for himself or others, must in the first place be in the state of grace; that is, God's friend: for how can God be pleased at the doings of His mortal enemies? How can He relish or approve actions which proceed from a heart invenomed with the deadly poison of mortal sin? * Could I work miracles, and wanted but a grain of true charity; all this, says St. Paul,† were but wind, it were all unprofitable. Next unto this, he must not fail to have an intention of doing such a good work to relieve the soul, which either he names himself, or leaves to God's determination and choice. Besides, the work must be good and virtuous of itself; that is, accompanied with all due circumstances. The more

* Some theologians, however, of no small weight, hold a contrary opinion, as regards the gaining Indulgences for the souls in Purgatory. Both may be stated as probable. See what the author himself says, a little below.

† 1 Cor. xiii. 2.

love, humility, contrition, and devotion you bring, and
the more penal your work is, the more precious will it
be in the sight of God, and the greater miracles will
it do in Purgatory; rejoicing the afflicted souls,
quenching their flames, and converting Purgatory into
Paradise.

But let us now look a little into the consequence of
this doctrine. Does it not hence follow, that all evil
and ungodly priests are unprofitably employed for the
good of the souls? for, since they are supposed to be
in a damnable condition, all they do seems to be as
good as nothing: and then, what a world of Masses
shall we have quite cast away, what a world of foundations utterly lost; since they may often fall into such
wicked hands! Away with these discourses; which
are not only false, but very prejudicial to Purgatory.
Good divinity teaches that a Mass is always a Mass,*
always good, and of an infinite value: that the priest
that says it, or sings it, as a minister of God's Church,
let him be never so unworthy, is always acceptable for
her sake in whose name he acts; that, if you take him
as a private and particular person, it is true, all his
prayers and devotions can avail nothing; but, as he
represents the Church, he cannot fail to do the main
deed we have in view; and we need not scruple it.
You would be amazed, should I further tell you, that
it may happen sometimes, that you may gain more, by
hearing the Mass of an unworthy priest, than of
another; for that which is common to both is, that
they both offer up the propitiatory sacrifice of the
Mass, which is always pleasing in the sight of God:

* Suarez, d. 48, sec. 8.

they are both ministers of the Church, and, under this qualification, they are both acceptable persons; both have the intention you require, of relieving the soul you recommend unto them; both perform all the holy rites and ceremonies, which the Church prescribes in this case. In this they differ; that the one adds particular devotions of his own, which are grateful to God, because he is in the state of grace, and one of His adopted children; whereas the other's personal actions are of no worth, because we suppose him to be in a ill state. Well; but this is the cause why you, that know it, and are fearful to lose by the bargain, bring so many theological acts of faith, hope, and charity of your own, so many holy affections, springing from a zealous devotion, all inflamed with the love of God; that the loss you were afraid of is abundantly compensated, and with no little advantage to your cause. Be not then of the number of those mistaken persons, who profess they are afraid to found obits for their deceased kindred, least the Masses should come to be said by ungodly and irreligious priests. It were mere simplicity to be afraid of clear crystal water, because, forsooth, it issues out of the snout of a black marble serpent, or passes through the jaws of a lion of brass. Would you refuse a million of gold, if it were sent you out of Turkey from some wicked renegade? Or should the Pope send you a Cardinal's cap, would you be so squeamish as not to accept it, because the messenger that brought it were an ill-conditioned fellow? Elias was not so dainty as to forbear his meat because it was brought by a raven. Do, in God's Name, what is fitting; and leave the rest to God, who out of His infinite goodness knows how to supply all these defects; especially such as happen against your will, and such as you know not how to prevent, unless you were a prophet.

§ 4.—*Of the particular ways we have to help them.*

The holy Canons and Doctors of the Church comprehend all the means and advantages we have to relieve the dead, under these four general heads. (1) The priests' oblations and sacrifices; (2) the prayers of devout people; (3) alms-deeds; (4) fasting; under which you must include all kind of austerities, all penal works that afflict the body, what way soever; and, in a word, all that goes under the common notion of suffrages.

For the enjoying of all which helps, St. Augustine observes, how greatly it may import to bury the dead in churches where the bodies of Saints and holy martyrs lie interred: not that the mere lying there can so much avail them; but for this, that devout people resorting more thither than to other places, to perform their devotions to God and His Saints, and seeing the tombs of their deceased friends, cannot but remember to apply their charitable suffrages for the help of such needy persons.

I am in love with that religious practice of Bologna; where, upon funeral days, they cause hundreds and thousands of Masses to be said for the soul departed, in lieu of other superfluous and vain ostentations.

They stay not for the anniversary, nor for any other set day; but instantly do their best to release the poor soul from her torments, who must needs think the year long, if she must stay for help till her anniversary day appears. They do not, for all this, despise the laudable customs of the Church; they bury their friends with honour; they clothe great numbers of poor people; they give liberal alms; but, as there is nothing so certain, nothing so efficacious, nothing so divine, as the holy Sacrifice of the Mass, they fix their whole affection there, and strive all they can to relieve, the souls this way; and are by no means so lavish, as the fashion is, in other idle expenses and inopportune feastings, which are often more troublesome to the living than comfortable to the dead.

But you may not only comfort the afflicted souls by procuring Masses for them, nor yet only by offering up your prayers, fasts, alms-deeds, and such other works of piety; but you may bestow upon them all the good you do, and all the evil you suffer, in this world. If you offer up unto God all the cruel frettings and gripings you endure in a fit of the stone, which tears up your very entrails; if all the bitter sting and gnawings of the raging gout, when it buries you alive in a kind of Purgatory; if all the sensible tearings of a desperate megrim, when it cleaves your head in pieces; if the sullen humour of a quartan ague, which steeps your very heart in the gall of a deep melancholy; if all the other evils which murder you alive, and do not kill you outright, to be still killing you with a lingering death; if, I say, you offer up unto God all that causes you any grief or affliction, for the present relief of the poor languishing souls, you cannot believe what ease and comfort they will find by it. And as, in the buckets of a well, while the one sinks down to the bottom the other mounts up to the top, so the lower you humble yourself in your sufferings, the higher you will raise the souls in their flight towards heaven. Nor will you have cause to fear forgetting yourself, while you satisfy for them ; for it will infallibly come to pass, as St. John Chrysostom assures us, that God, who is always prodigal of His mercies, will be sure to remember you : and the holy souls, soaring up to heaven with the wings of your charity, will there plead for you with so much eloquence, as to gain your cause ; or at least obtain so much patience for you, as to defy the worst of your evils which do so insult and tyrannize over you with so much insolence. Pliny would make us believe there are certain fishes, that entertain so fair an amity and faithful correspondence with one another, that if one of them chance to be hung in the net, the other strives all he can possibly to set him free; and, having no other means to compass his design, presents his, his tail, or one of his fins, which the other lays fast hold on with his teeth, so that, while the one thrusts with all his might, and the other draws with all his force, they break the mesh, make way for the prisoner to get out, and so swim away, both triumphing in their liberty. Meanwhile, the kind fish that was sorely bitten, bleeds fresh of his wounds; and yet is so well pleased to have purchased his friend's liberty, though at the cost of his blood, that he thinks not of his own mischief, for the joy he takes in his friend's safety.

Do you the same for your friends, who are detained captives in Purgatory: lend them your arms, your head, your blood, all your griefs and pains, and they will be the sooner released out of their miserable thraldom; and you, by their favour, shall in your turn pass through it with so much swiftness, that you shall scarce feel the scorching flames, with which they are so grievously tormented.

You have another easy but most powerful means to help these unfortunate souls; and that is, to dispense out liberally amongst them the inexhaustible treasure of Indulgences; to cause Masses to be often said at privileged altars; to gain jubilees and other plenary Indulgences, which are applicable to the benefit of deceased souls. For, though some extravagant writers have been so bold, in their unwary speculations upon this subject, as to question whether the Pope's power in granting jubilees and other pardons, reach to Purgatory, or be only confined to this world, yet the current of sober Doctors must bear the sway, who all conclude that, as to the living, His Holiness proceeds by way of absolution, and, as to the dead, by way of suffrages and satisfactions; but has full power over both, to loose or bind, open or lock up heaven's gates, and to distribute the treasure of the Church; and that he has his commission for all this from the sacred mouth of Jesus Christ Himself.* Certainly, there be thousands who deserve to lie in Purgatory, were it only for this strange neglect, that, having so rich a treasure in their hands wherewith to ransom poor captive souls, they were so careless as to

* St. Matt. xvi. 19.

make little or no use of it; but let a thousand occasions slip, in which they might have released them, and all for want of a little pains to gain Indulgences.

And they are the less to be excused, because it is very probable that they may gain Indulgences, which are applicable to the dead, whether they be in the state of grace or no, so they do but the work prescribed.*

"What shall they do," says the Apostle, "that are baptized for the dead?"† What means this baptism for the dead? I leave a dozen of interpretations, to tell you there were some fervent Christians in those days that took a world of pains, and suffered a world of austerities, for the faithful departed ; and so were baptised in the tears of contrition, and in the blood of a most rigorous and penitential life. I require not so much of you ; only a little care of applying such Indulgences as you have in your power, to do them good, who, by a little of your favourable assistance, would be soon set at liberty. Cruel heart! canst thou refuse so slight a courtesy to souls so holy, and yet in so lamentable a condition? And, if thou hast the honour to get in thither thyself, hereafter—I say, the honour—dost thou not deserve to be let alone, to feel at leisure the smart of thy idleness and disloyalty? Who will take the pains to help a wretch, who would scarce stir a finger to help out souls whose eternal happiness he might as easily have procured, as cut a small thread in two, or quench a little spark of fire?

Prepos. de Indulg. q. 14, dub. 10, et alii. passim.
† I Cor. xv. 29.

I have not the confidence to propose things of greater hardship ; and therefore I will not exhort you to imitate the example of St. Catharine of Siena, who offered to suffer the pains of Purgatory itself, in place of her dear mother; nor that of St. Catharine of Genoa, who really suffered two years together what flesh and blood is not able to endure in this mortal life ; nor that of St. Christina the Wonderful, whose excesses in this kind were incredible, if not attested by very credible persons.* I know, there is no persuading you to devote yourself to such holy excesses ; lest you should chance to be taken at your word, as some others have been. I hope at least I may, without offence, remind you not to hold back from applying in this way all your fasts, hair-girdles, disciplines, and other corporal afflictions ; and, in a word, all the evils you suffer in body or soul, whether they be voluntary or unavoidable. This I beg, as a most welcome alms to the poor souls in Purgatory, and a charity which will be of no little comfort to yourself. Do but as Magdalene and Martha did, when they saw their brother Lazarus locked up underground, and overwhelmed with earth. They wept and took on so bitterly, that they drew tears from our Blessed Saviour, and rescued their brother out of the jaws of death. They are your brothers, whom I entreat for ; they are prisoners underground ; Christ Jesus has as tender a Heart as ever : give yourselves, then, to acts of contrition ; let a tear steal now and then from your eyes ; and haply sweet Jesus will be so well pleased to see them, that they may suffice to quench the flames of Purgatory; and possibly work a miracle there, in raising souls to life everlasting, and placing them above the firmament, that lie now, as it were, buried in that subterraneous lake of fire. But, if you be so arid and barren, so niggardly, as not to afford them a tear, at least send them the sweet refreshment of a devout aspiration, or some short but vigorous ejaculatory prayer, which, as a fiery dart, you may be still levelling at the Heart of Almighty God. Give them a good thought, or a cordial expression of sorrow, that you are not able to afford them the relief you could wish. Do never so little, so you do it with a good heart, and you will assuredly give them much ease in their implacable torments. The people of God were condemned to be cruelly massacred, or destroyed by fire, when Queen Esther, fetching but a deep sigh or two, and whispering but a few words into the ear of King Assuerus, did so charm him as to work the redemption of above a million of souls, who must otherwise have been delivered over to the fury of fire and sword. Are you so void of charity, or is the blood that runs in your veins, and feeds your heart, so frozen up, as not to yield one drop of compassion for God's people, who are most miserably handled by a most cruel inundation of Purgatory fire? If so, let us conclude that nature was deceived; for, thinking to make you a man, she missed her aim, and made you a very tiger, void of all humanity and common civility.

It was a pious invention, that of certain bishops and other ecclesiastical persons of Rome, A.D. 984,[*]

[*] Baronius, *An.* 987.

to erect a sodality of those that should particularly devote themselves to pray for the dead : which custom continued a long time at Rome, and is yet extant in some parts of the Christian world. When one of their number dies, they all contribute their pious labours to help him out of Purgatory. I say, all; not only those who remain yet alive, but those also who are already got into heaven ; so that it is impossible for him to make any long stay there. What a pleasure it is, to see that a soul of this happy confraternity does no sooner enter into Purgatory, but a good part of heaven and earth conspires to procure his enlargement ! This is to be wise indeed ; these are matters of state, which all the world should be well versed in, as importing them far more than the government of whole kingdoms. Methinks, you that read this should now long to spread abroad this most excellent devotion, by erecting one of these sodalities, which would be of so great advantage to yourself and others. Most part of mankind is so taken up with building rich houses, or providing stately tombs for their rotten carcasses, they have no leisure to think what will become of their souls, or in what a fiery mansion they are like to be lodged at their first appearance in the other world. Do they not in truth deserve to lie there, frying whole years, without mercy ? they that had so little understanding, as not to endeavour the avoiding of an evil which alone deserves the name, if compared with the petty evils of this world, which are such bug-bears in our weak-sighted apprehensions. A man that is undone by some cheat or surprise, may be pitied ; but he that sees his own ruin, and will not stir a foot to prevent it, no creature can pity such a man; and certainly, he deserves not the least compassion.

The world has generally a great esteem of Monsieur d'Argenton, Philip Commines; and many worthily admire him for the great wisdom and sincerity he has laboured to express in his whole history. But, for my part, I commend him for nothing more than for the prudent care he took here for the welfare of his own soul in the other world. For, having built a goodly chapel at the Augustins in Paris, and left them a good foundation, he tied them to this perpetual obligation, that they should no sooner rise. from table, but they should be sure to pray for the rest of his precious soul. And he ordered it thus, by his express will; that one of the religious should first say aloud: Let us pray for the soul of Monsieur d'Argenton; and then all should instantly say the psalm *De profundis.* Gerson lost not his labour, when he took such pains to teach little children to repeat often these words: My God, my Creator, have pity on your poor servant, John Gerson. For these innocent souls, all the while the good man was dying, and after he was dead, went up and down the town with a mournful voice, singing the short lesson he had taught them, and comforting his dear soul with their innocent prayers.

Now, as I must commend their prudence who thus wisely cast about how to provide for their own souls, against they come into Purgatory, so I cannot but more highly magnify their charity, who, less solicitous for themselves, employ their whole care to save others

out of that dreadful fire.   And sure I am, they can
lose nothing by the bargain, who dare thus trust God
with their own souls, while they do their uttermost to
help others : nay, though they should follow that un-
paralleled example of F. Hernando de Monsoy,* of
the Society of Jesus, who, not content to give away all
he could from himself to the poor souls, while he lived,
made them his heirs after death ; and by express will
bequeathed them all the Masses, rosaries, and whatsoever else should be offered for him by his friends
upon earth.

§ 5.—*Certain questions resolved, about the appli-cation and distribution of our suffrages.*

It will not be amiss here to resolve you certain
pertinent questions.   Whether the suffrages we offer
up unto God shall really avail them for whom we offer
them : and whether they alone, or others also, may
receive benefit by them ?   Whether it be better to pray
for a few at once, or for many, or for all the souls
together ?   And for what souls in particular ?

To the first I answer ; if your intention be to help
any one in particular, who is really in Purgatory, so
your work be good, it is infallibly applied to the party
upon whom you bestow it.   For, as divines teach, it
is the intention of the offerer which governs all ; and
God, of His infinite goodness, accommodates Himself
to the petitioner's request, applying unto each one,
what has been offered for his relief.   If you have
nobody in your thoughts, for whom you offer up your

* *Rho. Hist.* l. i. c. 4, sec. 3

prayers, they are only beneficial to yourself; and what would be thus lost for want of application, God lays up in the treasury of the Church, as being a kind of spiritual waif, or stray, to which nobody can lay any just claim. And, since it is the intention which entitles one to what is offered, before all others, what right can others pretend to it; or with what justice can it be parted, or divided amongst others, who were never thought of?

And hence I take my starting-point to resolve your other question; that if you regard their best advantage whom you have a mind to favour, you had better pray for a few, than for many together: for, since the merit of your devotions is but limited, and often in a very small proportion, the more you divide and subdivide it amongst many, the lesser share comes to every one in particular. As if you should distribute a crown, or an angel,* amongst a thousand poor people, you easily see your alms would be so inconsiderable, they would be little better for it: whereas, if it were all bestowed upon one or two, it were enough to make them think themselves rich.

Now, to define precisely, whether it be always better done, to help one or two souls efficaciously, than to yield a little comfort to a great many, is a question I leave for you to exercise your wits in.

I could fancy it to be your best course to do both; that is, sometimes to single out some particular soul, and to use all your powers to lift her up to heaven · sometimes, again, to parcel out your favours upon

---

* A gold coin of that period, so called because it was stamped with the image of an angel.

many ; and, now and then, also to deal out a general
alms upon all Purgatory.   And you need not fear
exceeding in this way of charity, whatsoever you
bestow ; for you may be sure nothing will be lost by
it.   And St. Thomas will tell you, for your comfort,
that since all the souls in Purgatory are perfectly
united in charity, they rejoice exceedingly when they
see any of their whole number receive such powerful
helps as to dispose her for heaven.   They every one
take it as done to themselves, whatsoever is bestowed
upon any of their fellows, whom they love as themselves : and, out of a heavenly kind of courtesy, and
singular love, they joy in her happiness, as if it were
their own.   So that it may be truly said, that you .
never pray for one or more of them, but they are all
partakers, and receive a particular comfort and satisfaction by it.

Methinks, this very consideration should enkindle
in your hearts a fresh desire to be often solacing those
happy souls, and to entitle yourselves their special
benefactors, who will never suffer the remembrance
of your tender mercies to be blotted out of their
grateful memories.

But let us now state the case thus.   Suppose you
should employ another to do those good works for
the souls, will they have the same effect as if you had
done them yourself?   Again, should this other, whom
you thus employ, be an ungracious fellow, would all his
endeavours be able to give any ease to the souls for
whose sakes you procure them?   I am so taken with
the angelical. doctrine of St. Thomas, that I will go no
further for an answer.   He tells us, then, that if you

be good, and that other be stark nought, by whom
you procure the dirge, for example, to be said, or
any other good work to be performed, that can be
performed, that can be done by a third person—for
there be some that be personal—it does not at all
wither the fruit of your devotion, not obstruct the
soul's benefit for whom you procured it :—that, if he
chance to be good, so much the better ; the benefit
will be the greater ; though God look more upon the
chief agent, and principal cause, than upon the
accessory or instrument He thinks fit to make use
of :—that, if you be wicked yourself, and the other
good, the good work will have its effect, and the
soul will be assisted by it :—that, if you should be
both so unhappy, as to be neither of you in the state
of grace (excepting Mass only, which can never fail
of its effect), all other means you use will be utterly
void, and of no effect ; because they proceed from so
ungrateful hands, and worse hearts. Would you have
God to accept of His enemies' presents ? and, while
you refuse to give Him your heart, to seal with His
Divine grace, would you have Him to deliver you
up His, to dispose of His mercies, for the benefit
of others ? No, wicked wretch ; no ! Till you alter
your condition, do not expect that God will appear
in His mercy, to bestow a jubilee on those holy souls
you entreat for. Nay, it falls out sometimes, even in
this world, that the pleading of an infamous advocate,
or a sworn enemy of the prince or State, makes the
criminal's case more odious and desperate ; and, in
lieu of a gibbet, procures him a wheel, or a worse
punishment. Yet I must tell you, and I must conjure

you, by all the obligations of humanity, that, be
you never so lost a creature, never so covered with
enormous crimes, you never fail at least to procure
Masses, and to distribute liberal alms for the relief
of the poor souls. And this for many reasons.

First; because the Mass is always to good purpose,
as having its effect, *ex opere operato,* as the school-
men speak ; or of itself, without any relation had
to him that says it, or causes it to be said.

Secondly ; because it is agreed that the last whole-
some advice we ought to give to a desperate soul,
plunged over head and ears in sin, is, to be sure
always to be good to the poor ; for, sooner or later,
good will come of it.

Thirdly ; it is truly said of alms-deeds, that they are
good solicitors, and have a most charming rhetoric,
to obtain of God, and to extort, as it were, out of
His Hands, what they please. Insomuch that, if
the sentence of condemnation were already signed
in the hands of God, it is the expression of St. Chrysologus,* God Himself would tear it to pieces, and
revoke the sentence, rather than refuse any favour
to the merciful. "Give alms," says the Holy Ghost,
"and hide it in the bosom of the poor; and your alms
will intercede for you."† So that, although you,
wicked wretch, cannot say a good prayer for the
souls,‡ yet your charity will supply your place, and
plead for you : and the poor that partake of it will
also pray for you ; and all this may possibly be to
good purpose. What your tongue cannot, your hand
will perform, with greater advantage; and what cannot

* *Serm.* viii.   † Ecclus. xxix.   ‡ But see above, p. 120.

proceed from your heart, which is poisoned with deadly sin, will out at your purse, which is full of mercy ; and will help to purchase some comfortable refreshment, to take off the fury of those hungry flames which are incessantly preying upon the poor souls.

And here again, taking upon me to be proctor for this suffering commonwealth, I conjure you to be liberal in distributing your alms, and procuring Masses for the souls departed. I can expect no less but that their Guardian Angels, or yours, or those of the poor, will inspire them with good thoughts, and move them to pour out their ardent and innocent prayers for you, in recompense of so great a charity. Meanwhile, you shall be like the crow that brought bread to St. Paul the Hermit, without so much as tasting it ; or like the whale that conveyed Jonas safe to the shore, without feeding on him ; or, to use St. Gregory's comparison, you shall be like the water in the Sacrament of Baptism, which, falling upon the head of a child, washes away the foul stain of original sin, and entitles him heir to the kingdom of heaven, and meanwhile glides away into some noisome sink, and there turns to filth and corruption.

Now to the last query ; for what souls in particular we ought most to concern ourselves ? I answer briefly thus : (1) Without question, all obligations of kindred, promise, gratitude, rule, command, &c., are to be served in the first place. (2) You cannot do better than offer up your devotions for those souls which are dearest to God, or His Blessed Mother.

(3) It is a singular charity to remember those that are in most need, or most neglected. (4) It is a pious and laudable piece of spiritual craft, to do for those that will be soonest released; for by this means you shall send into heaven good store of powerful advocates, who will incessantly plead for you, before the throne of mercy.

§ 6.—*How dangerous it is to trust others with what concerns the sweet rest of our souls in the next world.*

As I cannot but highly magnify and extol their charity, that have a solicitous care to rescue out of Purgatory the souls of their dear parents, friends, and acquaintance, so I cannot forbear deploring, and even laughing, at their folly and utter madness, as I may rightly term it, that leave all to the discretion of the heirs and friends they leave behind them. They must pardon me if I wrong them: it is the zeal of their good which transports me; it is a just indignation that sets my heart all on fire, to see how the wisest often prove the veriest fools in this occasion, which is the most important of all others. How many wills never see any other light but that of the fire which consumes them to ashes? How many false ones are daily forged, to fill up the others' room? How few do we see at this day punctually performed; or, rather, how many do we see not performed at all? Having procured a Mass or two of requiem, and the dirge to be said, for decency' sake, and for the honour of their house, who is there, almost, that

will give himself any further trouble to pray even
for his parents? The good man is scarce cold in
his grave, but his children fall together by the ears,
run into endless suits, seize upon what they can next
lay their hands on, right or wrong, and will not be
persuaded to forego it, but by main force of law, or
by the terror of dreadful excommunications. One
lays injustice to his father's charge, for doing so
much to advance his eldest son's fortune; another
cries, Out upon him for being so unnatural as to
undo his own child. The daughters think it hard
their portions are no greater; the whole house is
up in arms, and in continual alarms; and, in a word,
there is nothing but a mere confusion and hurly-burly
amongst them. Meanwhile, the good man has leisure
enough to sit at his task of suffering, and to lie frying
in Purgatory : not so much as one of his children
thinks on him, unless it be to brand him with some
injurious reproach. The unfortunate soul almost
killed himself with care, and had like also to have
damned himself, to make his children happy in this
world : and these barbarous harpies are so insatiable
as to be raking at the bones, and gnawing at the
very heart of their deceased father, who must needs
be very sensible,* if he know it, to see himself so
undutifully regarded by his own children. I will
bring him in, anon, to speak for himself, as best
able to hold forth his own lamentable condition;
and sure it will break your very heart to hear him.
And yet, tell me seriously, does he not deserve
all this, who might so easily, when time was, have

* *i.e.* Must needs feel it very keenly.

provided better for himself, and prevented all this
mischief, by obliging the Church to offer up good
store of Masses for him ; and who was so imprudent
as to leave it wholly to the discretion of his heirs
and executors, who are little better than direct barbarians? For is there any likelihood they will stir
to help him out of Purgatory ; they that cannot
afford him a stone upon his grave, worth a crown,
with a little inscription to put good people in mind
who lies there, that they may cast a good thought
after him ? But I shall have occasion yet to enlarge
myself more upon this subject ; and to make it appear
what an irreparable folly is committed, by the wisest
in the world, in neglecting one of the most important
affairs in their whole life.

It would go hard with many, were it true that a
person who neglected to make restitution in his lifetime, and only charged his heirs to do it for him in
his last will and testament, shall not stir out of Purgatory till restitution be really made ; let there be never
so many Masses said, and never so many satisfactory
works offered up for him. And yet St. Bridget, whose
revelations are for the most part approved by the
Church, hesitates not to set this down for a truth
which God had revealed unto her. Nor are there
wanting grave divines that countenance this rigorous
position, and bring for it many strong reasons and
examples, which they take to be authentical : and
the law itself, which says, that if a man do not restore
another's goods, there will always stick upon his soul
a kind of blemish, or obligation of justice. And since
the fault lies wholly at his door, he cannot, say they,

have the least reason to complain of the severity of God's justice, but must accuse his own coldness and extreme neglect of his own welfare. Nay, even those that are of the contrary persuasion, yet maintain that it is not only much more secure, but far more meritorious, to satisfy such obligations while we live, than to trust others with it, let them be never so near and dear unto us ; let it be your child, or your wife, or the very half of yourself, yet you ought not to trust your other half in this case, where we see men are so daily cozened in their expectations. And you, that read this, and think to take so good order, that the like inconveniences cannot befall you, let me tell you, you are like to be one of the first that will be thus miserably cheated ; and perhaps far worse than your neighbours, if you do not seek to discharge all these obligations while you are yet alive, and rather to-day than to-morrow. And, I beseech you, take the pains once more to read over this section. For it is unto you I direct my speech ; or rather, it is God that speaks to you by my mouth. If you fail in it, you will have cause to repent ; for my part, I hold myself discharged.

But now, to return from whence I have a little digressed, I told you that these last authors, though they do not believe that a soul shall be necessarily bound to dwell in Purgatory fire till restitution be made, yet they hold that it may accidentally fall out, that she may be kept there far longer than she would have been otherwise. For the creditors, who have received their due, the poor you have made amends to, for what was wrongfully taken from them, and others, well satisfied with your just proceedings, will make it their business to pray for your soul; for want of whose prayers you may lie, God knows how long, neglected and forgotten, in that fiery dungeon. And believe it, let the first opinion be never so improbable in your judgment, it will not be very safe for you to lie in Purgatory till the case be decided: nor will it be your wisest course to learn there how egregiously you have played the fool, in not clearing your debts sooner, and providing better for the ease of your soul. I am clearly of the second opinion; but would advise you to make use of the first: that the one serving you as a bridle, the other may be as a spur, to incite you to that which doth more import you than the dominion of the whole world. You would be loth to be Emperor of the universe, upon condition to be perpetually tormented with the stone, or the gout, or to lie broiling upon a gridiron. And are you so wilfully unwary as to cast yourself into the flames of Purgatory, upon a vain confidence that your friends or your children will fetch you out, who perhaps have scarce a thought of you once in a twelvemonth?

You have no reason in the world to expect others should love you better than you love yourself: so that if you can find in your heart to neglect yourself, it is a folly to expect others will have more care of you. Sure it is not good to go to heaven by proxy; nor to be beholden to another's courtesy, in what concerns the necessary refreshment and ease of our souls. You that are so rich in worldly wealth, but bare enough of solid virtue, give but a tolerable excuse why you do not build a chapel or an hospital; that good people, remembering their founder, may be daily pouring out their prayers for you, both living and dead. That which you often cast away at an unlucky throw at dice, would be sufficient. That which you bury in a capricious piece of building, or devour at an idle entertainment, were more than enough. Why do not you get a privileged altar in your own parish; or at least cause frequent Masses to be said at such altars, to release poor souls, that others may be as kind to you hereafter? Why do not you send good store of alms to poor prisoners, that your charity may help to redeem souls out of Purgatory? You do nothing of all this, and yet would be thought to be in your right senses: which I look upon, for my part, as a mere paradox.

§ 7.—*Some motives, fetched even as far as the other world, to stir us up to be mindful of the dead.*

Cardinal Cajetan has a singular tenet, which will not a little help to promote piety, and deserves highly to be recorded, as a doctrine which suits well with the infinite goodness of our most just and merciful God. The question is, what becomes of all the merit of those Masses, and other suffrages, which are offered for souls which are not in Purgatory? Some hold, it is applied to their parents, alliance, or friends; others, to those that are so friendless as to have nobody to remember them; others, to them that stand in most need of help; others will have it hoarded up with the rest of the Church's treasure. But this learned

Cardinal maintains that it goes all to relieve their souls, who in this world were particularly addicted to pray for the dead. And what can be more reasonable? According to the measure we deal out to others, it shall be measured to us again.* "Give, and it shall be given to you," says Almighty God.†

Who can lay a better claim to it then they? For, first, the founders themselves, were they but half acquainted with what passes in the other world, cannot but be well pleased at it. Then, it is a powerful incentive to increase devotion in the hearts of all good Christians, who may hope in their turns to reap the like fruit of their charitable labours, for the good of souls. And who can find fault, that such straggling suffrages, which of right belong to nobody, should be so profitably employed? This opinion is no article of faith; but it is a very pious conjecture, worthy of that most eminent Cardinal. And methinks I see the blessed souls themselves, for whom these holy suffrages were offered, to lie prostrate before the throne of God, beseeching Him to apply them to those needy souls, who while they lived were so full of charity as to forget themselves, to be sure to remember them.

Methinks I see the other Saints in heaven, who were handed out of Purgatory by the arms of charity, to be joint-petitioners, and their good Angels also; and all of them together to become earnest suitors to obtain this favour of Almighty God, who is easily overcome in a suit of this nature; which is so rational, that the granting it must needs extol His ineffable

* St. Matt. vii. 2.　　　　† St. Luke vi. 38.

wisdom and mercy. And I cannot but think, that if the case were to be decided by the souls in Purgatory, they would all unanimously agree that such suffrages as these, which out of mere ignorance were misapplied to those that could make no benefit of them, cannot be better disposed of than to their companions, who in their lifetime were so charitable to other souls. This I take to be a very moving consideration; and yet I have just cause to fear, all I can say to you will hardly suffice to mollify that hard heart of yours; and therefore my last refuge shall be to set others on, though I call them out of the other world.

And first, let a damned soul read you a lecture, and teach you the compassion you ought to bear to your afflicted brethren. Remember how the rich glutton in the gospel,* although he was buried in hell-fire, took care for his brothers who survived him; and besought Abraham to send Lazarus back into the world, to preach and convert them, lest they should be so miserable as to come into that place of torments. A strange request for a damned soul! and which may shame you, that are so little concerned for the souls of your brethren, who are in so restless a condition.

In the next place, I will bring in the soul of your dear father, or mother, to make her own just complaints against you. Lend her, then, a dutiful and attentive ear; and let none of her words be lost: for she deserves to be heard out, while she sets forth the state of her most lamentable condition. Peace! It is a holy soul, though clothed in flames, that directs her speech to you after this manner.

* St. Luke xvi. 27, 28.

K

"Am I not the most unfortunate and wretched parent that ever lived? I that was so silly, as to presume that having ventured my life, and my very soul also, to leave my children at their ease, they would at least have had some pity on me, and endeavour to procure for me some ease and comfort in my torments? Alas; I burn insufferably, I suffer infinitely, and have done so, I know not how long; and yet this is not the only thing that grieves me. Alas, no! it is a greater vexation to see myself so soon forgotten by my own children, and so slighted by them, for whom I have in vain taken so much care and pains. Ah, dost thou grudge thy poor mother a Mass, a slight alms, a sigh, or a tear? Thy mother, I say, who would most willingly have kept bread from her own mouth, to make thee swim in an ocean of delights, and to abound with plenty of all worldly goods? See how proudly this unnatural child struts up and down, as fine as hands can make him, as glorious as the sun; while I, his poor mother, have no other robes left me but scorching flames of fire! See how he empties my coffers, to cast it upon his horses and dogs, or upon men worse than either; and cannot find the heart to lay out a penny in charitable uses for his poor mother! His gold flies about the table, as nimbly as the dice he plays with; and in mere sport and merriment he throws away that which cost me a world of pains, and perhaps was the occasion of my death, and my cruel confinement to this place of torments. He cannot afford me so much as a cup of cold water, wherewith to quench my flames; while he gluts himself with all superfluous and choice dainties. Am I not well served, for having had so little understanding, and so little of common sense in me, as to trust this hard heart, without a spark of good feeling in it, to have the slightest sense of my deplorable condition? Who will not refuse me comfort, when my own childen, my very bowels, do their best to forget me? What a vexation is it to me, when my companions in misery ask me whether I left no children behind me, and why they are so haggard-natured* as to neglect me? what can I say, or what answer can I make but this, that I thought I had brought forth children, but find them to be mere vipers and tigers? When I was upon my death-bed, struggling for life, these hypocritical children feigned themselves in despair: their pale looks, their counter-feit tears, their sighs, their sobs, their kind expres-sions, delivered in soft and smooth language, made me verily believe they loved me, and won me to play the fool thus, to rely upon them; when, God knows, they longed for nothing more than to close up my eyes, and were almost ready to burst for very grief that I died no sooner, that they might have sooner enjoyed the goods I had scraped together, with the hazard of my life, and poor soul too. I was willing to forget my own concerns, to be careful of theirs; and those ungrateful ones have now buried me in an eternal oblivion, and clearly left me to shift for myself in these dread tortures, without giving me the least ease or comfort. Oh, what a fool was I? had I given to the poor the thousandth part of those goods which I left this miserable child, I had long before this been

* A haggard was a wild, untamed hawk.

K 2

joyfully singing the praises of my Creator, in the choir of angels; whereas now I lie panting and groaning under excessive torments, and am like still to lie by it, for any relief that is to be looked for from this undutiful, ungracious child, whom I made my sole heir. Go, you mortals; go, hereafter, and trust your children, your kindred, and your heirs; that you may be treated by them as I am by my son, who was dearer to me than the very apple of my eye. Oh, it is the greatest piece of improvidence in the whole world, to rely upon the discretion of indiscreet or undutiful children, who would sooner be scuffling and tugging one another for a part of our inheritance, than striving to help us out of our pains. Sure, parents are either bewitched, or grown senseless, to hazard their souls for such untoward and ill-natured children, who have not a drop of good blood in their hearts, nor a grain of true filial love. But am I not all this while strangely transported, miserable that I am, thus to amuse myself with unprofitable complaints against my son; whereas indeed I have but small reason to blame any but myself? since it is I, and only I, that am the cause of all this mischief. For did not I know, that in the grand business of saving my soul, I was to have trusted none but myself? did I not know, that with the sight of their friends, at their departure, men use to lose all the memory and friendship they had for them? Did I not know, that God Himself had foretold us, that the only ready way to build ourselves eternal tabernacles in the next world, is not to give all to our children, but to be liberal to the poor? Did I not often hear it preached to me, that a cup of cold water sometimes happily bestowed, was sufficient to put out Purgatory fire? Did they not as often ring it in my ears, that a wise man sends his good works before him, and leaves them not for others to finish; as fools do, who by that means come to carry nothing with them but a shameful remorse, which lies like a viper at their breast, continually gnawing and devouring them? I cannot deny, then, but the fault lies at my door, and that I am deservedly thus neglected by my children. And, were I disposed to wish harm to anybody, I would wish them no greater mischief than that their children should serve them just as they have served me; I say, that my ungodly offspring may come hither, and be as much neglected and forgotten as I am; and see, when it is too late, what it is to trust to the kindness of children, which is commonly buried in the same grave with their parents. It is one of my greatest miseries, that I have not the face to beg any comfort of God in my sufferings. For, whereas He clearly promised me all favour, so I would but be good to the poor, I have done the clean contrary; putting more confidence in the uncertain performance of unworthy children, than in the infallible truth of God's word. The only comfort I have left me in all my afflictions is, that others will learn at my cost this clear maxim; not to leave to others a matter of so near concern, as the ease and repose of their own souls: but to provide for them carefully themselves. O God! how dear have I bought this experience; to see my fault irreparable, and my misery without redress!"

One must have a heart of steel, or no heart at all, to hear these sad regrets, and not feel some tenderness for the poor souls, and as great an indignation against those who are so little concerned for the souls of their parents and other near relations. I wish, with all my soul, that all those who shall light upon this passage, and hear the soul so bitterly deplore her misfortune, may but benefit themselves half as much by it, as a good prelate did when the soul of Pope Benedict VIII., by God's permission, revealed unto him her lamentable state in Purgatory.* For so the story goes; which is not to be questioned. This Pope Benedict appears to the Bishop of Caprea, and conjures him to go to his brother, Pope John, who succeeded him in the Chair of St. Peter, and to beseech him, for God's sake, to give great store of alms to poor people, to allay the fury of the fire of Purgatory, with which he found himself highly tormented. He further charges him to let the Pope know withal, that he did acknowledge, liberal alms; had already been distributed for that purpose; but had found no ease at all by it, because all the money that had been then bestowed was acquired unjustly, and so had no power to prevail before the just tribunal of God for the obtaining of the least mercy. The good bishop, upon this, makes haste to the Pope, and faithfully relates the whole conference that had passed between him and the soul of his predecessor; and with a grave voice and lively accent enforces the necessity and importance of the business; that, in truth, when a soul lies a burning, it is in vain to

* Baronius, *An.* 1024.

dispute idle questions: the best course, then, is to run instantly for water, and to throw it on with both hands, calling for all the help and assistance we can, to relieve her: and that His Holiness should soon see the truth of the vision by the wonderful effects which were like to follow. All this he delivers so gravely, and so to the purpose, that the Pope resolves out of hand to give in charity vast sums out of his own certain and unquestionable revenue; whereby the soul of Pope Benedict was not only wonderfully comforted, but questionless soon released of her torments. In conclusion, the good bishop, having well reflected with himself, in what a miserable condition he had seen the soul of a Pope who had the repute of a Saint, and was really so, it worked so powerfully with him, that quitting his mitre, crosier, bishopric, and all worldly greatness, he shut himself up in a monastery, and there made a holy end; choosing rather to have his Purgatory in the austerity of a cloister than in the flames of the Church suffering. I wish, again, they would in this but follow the example of King Louis of France, who was son to Louis the Emperor, surnamed the Pious. For they tell us* that this Emperor, after he had been thirty-three years in Purgatory, not so much for any personal crimes or misdemeanours of his own, as for permitting certain disorders in his empire, which he ought to have prevented, was at length permitted to show himself to King Louis his son, and to beg his favourable assistance: and that the King did not only most readily grant him his request, procuring Masses to be said in all the monas-

* Baronius, *An.* 874.

teries of his realm, for the soul of his deceased father, but drew thence many good reflections and profitable instructions, which served him all his lifetime after. Do you the same; and believe it, though Purgatory fire is a kind of baptism, and is so styled by some of the holy Fathers, because it cleanses a soul from all the dross of sin, and makes it worthy to see God, yet is it your sweetest course, here to baptize yourself frequently in the tears of contrition, which have a mighty power to wash away all the blemishes of sin; and so prevent in your own person, and extinguish in others, those baptismal flames of Purgatory fire, which are so dreadful.

THE FIFTH SURVEY.

HOW ALL ANTIQUITY WAS EVER DEVOTED TO PRAY FOR THE DEAD.

THIS charitable devotion for the dead is a thing so inbred and natural unto us all, that we seem, as it were, to suck it in with the very milk of our nurses : nor was there ever any people, I do not say Christian, but even Jewish, or heathenish, which did not profess some piety in this way.

As for the Jews, it is well known to be their constant practice this day, to pray for souls departed, and is confessed to be so by Purcas himself, and other modern protestants. And what their custom was, when they had the privilege of being the only chosen people of Almighty God, the Scripture itself bears witness ; especially where it relates the incomparable zeal which that valiant, invincible champion of heaven, Judas Machabeus,* had for the good of their souls, who had unfortunately been slain by their enemies. Take this story in brief, thus : Having in several fierce encounters made such a slaughter of his enemies, as to strew the field over with dead carcasses, and to stain the rivers with blood, he caused a diligent search to be made for all those that had fallen on his side, to have them honourably interred in the sepulchres of their fathers. But the mischief was, that in stripping them of their clothes,

* 2 Mach. xii.

they discovered under their coats some unlawful spoils which they ought to have destroyed, according to their law; but had secretly reserved to themselves: a crime for which, they all instantly concluded, those unfortunate souls had deservedly been cast away, and cut off by the hand of God. And some there were, doubtless, that fell a cursing this their sordid avarice and high transgression : but the good captain takes this occasion to exhort them to adore the just judgments of heaven, and to learn at the others' cost to have the fear of God before their eyes, and to be more religious in their ways; and yet withal to be more reserved in their censures, and rather to have pity on the souls of their fellow-soldiers, who probably might not die in so desperate a condition, as not to be relieved by their help. This done, he makes a collection: he raises a sum of twelve thousand drachms; he sends it to Jerusalem to procure sacrifices to be offered for their sins that were slain; who, for ought he knew, might die in a fair way to a hopeful resurrection. Now, which shall we first admire, the tender heart of this noble cavalier, or his religious piety, or his charitable liberality? He knew well, those miserable wretches had committed a foul crime; and yet he would not despair of their salvation : but was willing to believe they repented themselves of their frailty; and that God had sent them their deaths only as a temporal punishment, for the terror of others. Nor had he the least doubt but that our Lord would be well pleased with his charity, and accept of the sacrifices which he thus offered for the repose of their souls. And certainly, the fact is most highly commended by the sacred text; which concludes the story in these words : " It is therefore a holy and healthful cogitation to pray for the dead, that they may be loosed from their sins." Oh, that so fair an example would teach all Christians to be good and liberal to the dead ! For, alas ! the greatest part of mankind content themselves with drawing two or three sighs at a funeral, or saying a short prayer, or two at most : whereas this generous captain, even before the clear light of the gospel, did all this, and confirmed it with a noble gift of twelve thousand drachms.

§ 1.—*Of the natural instinct of all nations to honour and comfort the dead.*

It may well put most Catholics to the blush, to consider what an incredible care all nations have ever had of the dead, by the mere impulse of nature.

Cæsar takes notice* how superstitiously pious the ancient French were in this kind; who, together with the dead corpse, which they burnt upon a great pile of wood, were wont to consume all that had been precious and dear to him when he lived; as, all his rich moveables, his dogs, his horses, nay, sometimes his very servants also, who took it for a great honour that they might be suffered so to mingle their ashes with those of their dear lord and master. And does not the Roman history tell us,† that, when Otho the Emperor had stabbed himself with a dagger, many of his soldiers were seen to do the like, to show the affection they had for their prince, and how ready

---

* *De bello Gall.*   † Tacitus, *History.*

they were to sacrifice their lives for his honour and
service? I know, these customs were not only very
extravagant, but extreme rude and barbarous: and
yet they may serve to shame Christians, who are so
far from expressing any such love for the souls of
their friends, though they believe them to lie broiling
in Purgatory. For what would not these others have
done, or what would they not have given, to redeem
the souls of their friends out of cruel torments, had
they believed as much; since they were so prodigal
as to sacrifice their goods, and their very lives, to
their bare memories?

What shall I say of those other nations, whose
natural piety led them to place burning lamps at the
sepulchres of the dead, and strew them over with
sweet flowers, and odoriferous perfumes?* Do they
not put Christians in mind to remember the dead,
and to cast after them the sweet incense of their
devout sighs and prayers, and the perfumes of their
alms-deeds, and other good works?

It was very usual with the old Romans to shed
whole floods of tears, to reserve them in phial-glasses,
and to bury them with the urns, in which the ashes of
their dead friends were carefully laid up; and by them
to set lamps, so artificially composed as to burn without end. By which symbols they would give us to
understand, that neither their love, nor their grief,
should ever die; but that they would always be sure
to have tears in their eyes, love in their hearts, and
a constant memory in their souls for their deceased
friends. Good God! shall charity be overcome by

* Herod. lib. 2.

vanity? shall religion yield to idolatry, and shall the
Catholic Roman stoop to the Pagan Roman? shall
a little vainglory, or a mere natural affection, have the
power to draw whole glassfuls of tears from the eyes
of idolaters, and shall not a religious compassion
prevail so far as to draw a single tear, or a sigh, or a
good word, from the mouth of a Christian? shall they
take on so bitterly for dead carcasses, that are not
sensible of the flames that consume them; and shall
not we be more concerned for souls, that really feel
the smart of a most cruel fire? sure, they will one day
rise up in judgment against us, and reproach us for
believing as we do, and carrying ourselves clear contrary to the belief we profess.

They had another custom, not only in Rome, but
elsewhere, to walk about the burning pile, where the
dead corpse lay, and with their mournful lamentations
to keep time with the doleful sound of their trumpets;
and still, every turn, to cast into the fire some precious
pledge of their friendship. The women themselves
would not stick to throw in their rings, bracelets,
and other costly attires, nay their very hair also, the
chief ornament of their sex: and they would have
been sometimes willing to have thrown in both their
eyes, and their hearts too. Nor were there some
wanting, that in earnest threw themselves into the
fire, to be consumed with their dear spouses; so that
it was found necessary to make a severe law against
it: such was the tenderness that they had for their
deceased friends, such was the excess of a mere
natural affection. Now, our love is infused from

* Suet. in Aug. Dion. Alex.

heaven; it is supernatural, and consequently ought to be more active and powerful to stir up our compassion for the souls departed; and yet we see the coldness of Christians in this particular; how few there are that make it their business to help poor souls out of their tormenting flames.. It is not necessary to make laws to hinder any excess in this article; it were rather to be wished that a law were provided to punish all such ungrateful persons as forgot the duty they owe to their dead parents, and all the obligations they have to the rest of their friends.

It will help something to increase our confusion, to reflect how Alexander the Great behaved himself at the funeral of his dear Hephæstion.* They tell us, he spent at least twelve thousand talents, that is, above seven millions and two hundred thousand crowns, upon his funeral pile. It was beautified with a world of rich and goodly statues, made of ivory, ebony, or some precious metal: amongst others, you might have seen curious mermaids, with exquisite music locked up within them; eagles, dragons, and other beasts, represented to the life; stately galleries hung with scarlet richly embroidered; triumphant crowns of pure gold; torches fifteen cubits high; perfumes without end. Oh, what an excess of love, and superfluity, was this! what a stir, to make a handful of ashes of the carcass of a miserable wretch? And yet all this was nothing to the mad profuseness of that other infamous and desperate king,† who, while yet living, built his own funeral pile, and made himself, and a world of treasure, to the value of fifty millions of gold,

* Diod. Sic. l. 17, c. 16.   † Justin. l. 1. Diod. Sic. l. 3. Bud.

to be all consumed to ashes. What reflections shall we make upon all this; we that are scarce willing to spare a shilling to ease a soul that lies consuming in the flames of Purgatory?

Tell me, dear reader, what would they not have done for souls; they that bore so religious a respect to the bones, ashes, and small remainder of dead carcasses? They first clothed themselves with black cypress, washed their hands clean, quenched the fire with milk and wine; then they made a diligent search for the bones, carefully raking them up out of the ashes; they placed them in their bosoms, washed them with their tears and their choicest wines, dried them again, and lapped them up in their finest linen, covered them over with roses and other costly perfumes, and so reserved them in urns of glass, ivory, or porphyry; and could never think they had done enough for them. And can we Christians, with the eye of our faith, pierce the earth and see poor souls burning in Purgatory fire, and see them with dry eyes and with a frozen heart? Can we be so niggardly as to grudge them a little comfort, or refuse to cast on our wine, our milk, and our flowers; the wine of our charity, the milk of our innocency, and the flowers of our devout sighs and prayers, to help to quench their flames? Christ Jesus told the Jews, that the Queen of Saba would condemn them at the latter day; and I fear Queen Artemisia * will condemn us; forasmuch as, having built one of the seven miracles of the world in honour of her dear lord and husband, not content with this exterior demonstration of the dutiful affection

* Strabo. l. 14. Diod. l. 16.

she had for him, she took a strange resolution, to drink up his ashes and to lodge them in her heart; and so to make it good to the very letter, that man and wife are indeed but one flesh, one body and soul, have but one life, and can die but one death. What would she not have done to have lodged his soul in heaven; she that took such care to lodge his ashes in her breast? What have you to say for yourselves, you unkind wives; or what answer can you make, you unnatural children; when she shall question you, what care you took to provide a better mansion for the souls of your husbands or your parents, when they were lodged in the merciless flames of Purgatory fire? Sure, you are not sprung from that wicked race of barbarous people, who were wont to feast themselves with the flesh of their dead parents, and to justify the fact by saying that it was better their bodies should be their meat, than the meat of worms!* I know this brutishness does not reign amongst us at this present; but, alas! there is another, not unlike to it, which is much in fashion; for how many children gourmandize themselves with the riches of their parents, drink up the sweat of their brows, and devour their goods, without so much as dreaming what becomes of their souls; whether they broil in glowing fire, or starve in freezing cold? Cruel wretches! Is this the gratitude with which they honour their parents? Are they indeed children, or rather are they not direct vultures and tigers?

I should never make an end, should I go about here to reckon up all the religious expressions of

* Strabo. Val. Max.

charity, which the pagans are known to have made to their dead friends; and therefore I say nothing of the ten valiant captains that were slain,* for not fishing for the bodies of their soldiers, and causing them to be buried; which was a crime they held unpardonable. I say as little of that pious custom of the Athenians, who would confer no honour or dignity, but upon those who were well known to have been always very religious in burying their ancestors and honouring their tombs. I take no notice of a world of sacrifices, prayers, and ceremonies, which were constantly performed by the vestal virgins, priests, and whole pagan clergy; nor of the stately mausoleums, pyramids, colossuses, and other stately monuments, which were built in honour of the dead. It grieves me to the very heart to consider, that there are scarce any to be found in the whole world that make less reckoning of the dead than some loose and idle Christians: and I know not how to be better revenged on them† than to wish, that in punishment of their coldness and want of charity, they may be just so served by their successors, as they dealt with their predecessors. It is the least they deserve, for neglecting a piety which they might have learnt of the pagans, and of the very beasts themselves; for some have been so curious as to observe in the ants, that in their little cells they have not only a hall and a granary, but a kind of churchyard also, or a place deputed for burying of their dead.

Xenoph. l. 1, Pausan. l. 2.

† The author, of course, uses this expression as a mere figure of speech. He had already (p. 149) put more charitable sentiments into the mouth of a mother speaking from Purgatory.

§ 2.—*The constant practice of the Church in all ages, to pray for the dead.*

It is a pleasure to observe the constant devotion of the Church of Christ in all ages, to pray for the dead. And first, to take my rise from the Apostles' time, there are many learned interpreters, who hold that baptism for the dead, of which the Apostle speaks,* to be meant only of the much fasting, prayer, alms-deeds, and other voluntary afflictions, which the first Christians undertook for the relief of their deceased friends. But I need not fetch in obscure places to prove so clear an apostolical and early custom in God's Church.

You may see a set form of prayer for the dead pre-scribed in all the ancient liturgies of the Apostles.† Besides, St. Clement‡ tells us, it was one of the•chief heads of St. Peter's sermons, to be daily inculcating to the people this devotion of praying for the dead : and St. Denis§ sets down at large the solemn ceremonies and prayers, which were then used at funerals ; and receives them no otherwise than as apostolical tradi-tions, grounded upon the Word of God. And certainly, it would have done you good to have seen with what gravity and devotion that venerable prelate performed the divine office and prayer for the dead, and what an ocean of tears he drew from the eyes of all that were present.

* 1 Cor. xv. 29.
† Liturgia utriusque, S. Jacobi. S. Math. S. Marci. S. Clem.
‡ *Epist.* i.   § S. Dion. *Eccles. Hier.* c. 7.

Let Tertullian speak for the next age.* He tells us how carefully devout people in his time kept the anniversaries of the dead, and made their constant oblations for the sweet rest of their souls. Here it is, says this grave author, that the widow makes it appear whether or no she had any true love for her husband; if she continue yearly to do her best for the comfort of his soul. To neglect so necessary a piece of service were to tell the world how she joys in his death, and was certainly long since divorced from him in affection. Believe it, all love is not expressed in setting out the solemnities of a noble funeral, hanging rooms in black, and shutting out the sun at noonday, to lie buried in darkness; nor appearing abroad with coach and lackeys all in complete mourning; howling and crying, and the like; there is often more ceremony or vanity in all this, than love. It is all rather to amuse the world, than to benefit the poor soul; who, God knows, has more need of other helps than these vain shows of pride and ostentation. All the day long you do nothing but whine and cry, that your dear husband is gone, and has left you such a debt, and so great a charge of children to provide for, that you know not which way to turn yourself: and all this while it is not in your thoughts, what is become of this dear husband of yours, or what he suffers in the other world, and what need he has of better comfort than can spring from your unnecessary lamentations. Let your first care be, to ransom him out of Purgatory, and when you have once placed him in the empyrean heaven, he will be sure to take care for you and yours.

* Tertull. *De cor. mil.* c. 3; *De monogam.* c. 10.

L 2

I know your excuse is, that having procured for him the accustomed services of the Church, you need do no more for him ; for you verily believe he is already in a blessed state.   But this is rather a poor shift to excuse your own sloth and laziness, than that you believe it to be so in good earnest.   For there is no man, says Origen,* but the Son of God, can guess how long, or how many ages, a soul may stand in need of the purgation of fire.   Mark the word, *ages :* he seems to believe that a soul may, for whole ages, that is, for so many hundred years, be confined to this fiery lake, if she be wholly left to herself and her own sufferings.

It was not without confidence, says Eusebius,† of reaping more fruit from the prayers of the faithful, that the honour of our nation, and the first Christian Emperor, Constantine the Great, took such care to be buried in the Church of the Apostles, whither all sorts of devout people resorting to perform their devotions to God and His Saints, would be sure to remember so good an Emperor.   Nor did he fail of his expectation ; for it is incredible, as the same author observes, what a world of sighs and prayers were offered up for him upon this occasion.

St. Athanasius‡ brings an elegant comparison, to express the incomparable benefit which accrues to the souls in Purgatory by our prayers.   As the wine, says he, which is locked up in the cellar, yet is so recreated with the sweet odour of the flourishing

---

* Lib. 8 *in Rom.* c. 11.

† Euseb. lib. 4, c. 60, 71.   ‡ Q. 34 *ad Antiochum.*

vines, which are growing in the fields, as to flower afresh, and leap, as it were, for joy; so the souls that are shut up in the centre of the earth feel the sweet incense of our prayers, and are exceedingly comforted and refreshed by it.

We do not busy ourselves, says St. Cyril,* with placing crowns or strewing flowers at the sepulchres of the dead; but we lay hold on Christ, the very Son of God, who was sacrificed upon the Cross for our sins: and we offer Him up again to His Eternal Father in the dread Sacrifice of the Mass, as the most efficacious means to reconcile Him, not only to ourselves, but to them also.

St. Epiphanius† stuck not to condemn Arius for this damnable heresy amongst others, that he held it in vain to pray for the dead: as if our prayers could not avail them.

St. Ambrose‡ prayed heartily for the good Emperor Theodosius, as soon as he was dead; and made open profession that he would never give over praying for him, till he had by his tears and prayers conveyed him safe to the holy mountain of our Lord, whither he was called by his merits, and where there is true life everlasting.

He had the same kindness for the soul of the Emperor Valentinian,§ the same for Gratian, the same for his brother Satyrus and others; he promised them Masses, tears, prayers, and that he would never forget them, never give over doing charitable offices

---

* Orat. in fun. Valent.; et in fun. Satyr.
† *Heresi.*75.   ‡ St. Ambr. in Orat. in fun. Theodosii.
§ Cyril. Hieros. *in Catechesi* 5 *Mystag.*

for them. And much about this time it ̣was,* that
some, out of too much care that the dead should,
as soon as might be, have all the comfort they could
afford them, were grown into an abuse of making no
scruple of saying Mass for them after dinner; so that
the Church made a severe decree against it.

"Will you honour the dead?" says St. Chrysostom ;
"do not spend yourselves in unprofitable lamentations;
choose rather to sing psalms, to give alms, and to
lead holy lives. Do for them that which they would
willingly do for themselves, were they to return again
into the world: and God will accept it at your hands,
as if it came from them."

St. Augustine is everywhere very full of this subject;
but it may abundantly suffice here to set down a part
of the ardent prayer which he made for his good
mother, after her death. "Hearken to me, I beseech
Thee, O my God! for His sake who is the true
medicine of our wounds, who hung upon the Cross,
and, sitting at Thy right hand, makes intercession for
us. I know she has willingly, and from her heart,
forgiven such as offended her : forgive Thou also her
sins, O Lord ! forgive her, I beseech Thee, and enter
not with her into judgment. Let Thy mercy overtop
Thy justice, &c." "And I verily persuade myself that
Thou hast already done what I desire ; but yet accept,
O Lord, this prayer, which I willingly make. For
she, when the day of her death drew near upon her,
did not crave that her body might be sumptuously
adorned, or embalmed with spices and odours; nor
desired she any curious or choice monument, nor

* Conc. Carth. 3, can. 29.

cared she to be conveyed into her own country. They were not these things she recommended to us; but only she desired to be remembered at the altar, whereat she used to assist, without pretermission of any one day. Let her, therefore, rest in peace with her husband. And inspire, O Lord my God! inspire Thy servants, my brethren, that whosoever reads these my confessions, may at Thy altar remember Thy servant· Monica, with Patricius, her husband, &c."*

St. Paulinus, that charitable prelate who sold himself to redeem others, could not but have a great proportion of charity for captive souls in the other world. No; he was not only ready to become a slave himself, to purchase their freedom, but he became an earnest solicitor to others in their behalf; for in a letter to Delphinus, alluding to the story of Lazarus, he beseeches him to have at least so much compassion as to convey now and then a drop of water, wherewith to cool the tongues of poor souls that lie burning in the Church which is all a-fire.

I am astonished, when I call to mind the sad regrets of the people of Africa, when they saw some of their priests dragged away to martyrdom.† The author says, they flocked about them in great numbers, and cried out: "Alas! if you leave us so, what will become of us? who must give us absolution for our sins? who must bury us with the wonted ceremonies of the Church, when we are dead? and who will take care to pray for our souls?" Such a general belief

* *Confess.* lib. 9, c. 13.
† Victor Utic. lib. 2, *De persec. Wandal.*

they had in those days, that nothing is more to be
desired in this world, than to leave those behind us
who will do their best to help us out of our torments.

§ 3.—*A continuation of the same subject, from the sixth age after Christ unto our days.*

Almighty God has often miraculously made it
appear, how well He is pleased to be importuned by
us in the souls' behalf, and what comfort they receive
by our prayers. St. John Climacus writes,* that while
the monks were at service, praying for their good
Father Mennas, the third day after his departure,
they felt a marvellous sweet smell to rise out of his
grave, which they took for a good omen that his sweet
soul, after three days' purgation, had taken her flight
into heaven. For what else could be meant by that
sweet perfume, but the odour of his holy and innocent
conversation, or the incense of their sacrifices, and
prayers, or the primitial fruits of his happy soul,
which was now flown up to the holy mountain of
eternal glory, there enjoying the odoriferous and
never-fading delights of Paradise? Not unlike unto
this, is that story which the great St. Gregory relates
of one Justus, a monk.† He had given him up at first,
for a lost creature: but upon second thoughts, having
ordered Mass to be said for him for thirty days
together, the last day he appeared to his brother, and
assured him of the happy exchange he was now
going to make of his torments for the joys of heaven.

* In 4, gradu scalæ.   † *Dial.* c. 55, lib. 4.

Pope Symmachus* and his Council had reason to thunder out anathemas against those sacrilegious persons who were so frontless as to turn pious legacies into profane uses, to the great prejudice of the souls for whose repose they were particularly deputed by the founders. And certainly, it is a much fouler crime to defraud souls of their due relief, than to disturb dead men's ashes and to plunder their graves. And yet we read of dead carcasses, that have risen up in their graves, to struggle for their sheets with the wicked wretches who would have stolen them away. And it were to be wished, that more were permitted to do the like; and that souls might have leave to appear sometimes to those that abuse them so unconscionably! haply they might fright them into reason, who might not be otherwise persuaded to do them right.

St. Isidore† delivers it as an apostolic tradition, and general practice of the Catholic Church in his time, to offer up sacrifices and prayers, and to distribute alms, for the dead: and this, not for any increase of their merit, but either to mitigate their pains or to shorten the time of their durance.

Venerable Bede is a sure witness for the following century; whose learned works are full of wonderful stories, which he brings in confirmation of this Catholic doctrine and practice.

St. John Damascene‡ made an elegant oration, on purpose to stir up this devotion; where, amongst other

* 6 Synod. Rom.
† L. i. *De offic.* c. 18, and l. 2, c. penult.
‡ Orat. Quód ii qui, &c.

things, he says, it is impossible to number up all the
stories in this kind, which bear witness that the souls
departed are relieved by our prayers: and that otherwise God would not have appointed a commemoration
of the dead to be daily made in the unbloody Sacrifice
of the Mass, nor would the Church have so religiously
observed anniversaries and other days set apart for the
service of the dead.

Were it but a dog, says Simon Metaphrastes,* that
by chance were fallen into the fire, we should have so
much compassion for him as to help him out; and
what shall we do for souls who are fallen into
Purgatory fire? I say, souls of our parents and dearest
friends; souls that are predestinate to eternal glory,
and extreme precious in the sight of God? And
what did not the Saints of God's Church for them
in those days? some armed themselves from head to
foot in coarse haircloth; others tore off their flesh
with chains and rude disciplines; some, again, pined
themselves with rigorous fasts; others dissolved themselves into tears; some passed whole nights in contemplation; others gave liberal alms, or procured great
store of Masses; in fine, they did what they were
able, and were not well pleased that they were
able to do no more, to relieve the poor souls in
Purgatory. Amongst others, Queen Melchtild† is
reported to have purchased immortal fame for her
discreet behaviour at the death of the King her
husband; for whose soul she caused a world of
Masses to be said, and a world of alms to be dis-

* In *Vita St. Pachom. St. Euseb.* &c.
† Luitprand. l. 4, c. 7.

tributed, in lieu of other idle expences and fruitless lamentations.

There is one in the world, to whom I bear an immortal envy, and such an envy as I never mean to repent of. It is the holy Abbot Odilo; who was the author of an invention, which I would willingly have found out, though with the loss of my very heart's blood.

Reader, take the story as it passed; thus.* A devout religious man, in his return from Jerusalem, meets with a holy hermit in Sicily; he assures him, that he often heard the devils complain that souls were so soon discharged of their torments by the suffrages of the faithful, and particularly by the devout prayers of the monks of Cluny, who never ceased to pour out their prayers for them. This the good man carries to Odilo, then Abbot of Cluny; he praises God for His great mercy, in vouchsafing to hear the innocent prayers of his monks; and presently takes occasion to command all the monasteries of his Order, to keep yearly the commemoration of All Souls, next after the feast of All Saints. A custom which by degrees grew into such credit, that the Catholic Church thought fit to establish it all over the Christian world; to the incredible benefit of poor souls, and singular increase of God's glory. For who can sum up the infinite number of souls who have been freed out of Purgatory by this holy invention? or who can express the glory which accrued to this good abbot, who thus fortunately made himself procurator - general of the suffering Church, and furnished her people with such a con-

* Sigeb. in *Chron. an,* 998.

siderable supply of necessary relief, to alleviate the insupportable burthen of their sufferings?

St. Bernard* would triumph, when he had to deal with heretics that denied this privilege of communicating our suffrages and prayers to the souls in Purgatory. And with what fervour he would apply himself to this charitable employment of relieving poor souls, may appear by the care he took for good Humbertus,† though he knew him to have lived and died in his monastery so like a Saint, that he could scarce find out the fault in him which might deserve the least punishment in the other world; unless it were to have been too rigorous to himself, and too careless of his health: which in a less spiritual eye than that of St. Bernard, might have passed for a great virtue. But it is worth your hearing, that which he relates of blessed St. Malachy,‡ who died in his very bosom. This holy bishop, as he lay asleep, hears a sister of his, lately dead, making lamentable moan, that for thirty days together she had not eaten so much as a bit of bread. He starts up out of his sleep; and, taking it to be more than a dream, he concludes the meaning of the vision was to tell him, that just thirty days were now past since he had said Mass for her; as probably believing she was already where she had no need of his prayers. For this, indeed, is the ordinary excuse wherewith many use to cloak their idleness. "God be with him; he was a good soul: he is certainly in heaven, ere this; there is no more need to pray for him," &c.; whereas, God knows, heaven is

* *Serm. 66 in Cant.*
† *Serm. de obitu Humberti.*   ‡ In *Vita Malach.*

not so easily purchased as fools imagine. Howsoever, this worthy prelate so plied his prayers after this, that he soon sent his sister out of Purgatory ; and it pleased God to let him see, by the daily change of her habit, how his prayers had purged her by degrees, and and made her fit company for the Angels and Saints in heaven. For the first day, she was covered all over with black cypress; the next, she appeared in a mantle something whitish, but of a dusky colour : but the third day, she was seen all clad in white, which is the proper livery of the Saints. What think you now, says St. Bernard; is not the kingdom of heaven got by violence? Did not St. Malachy force it by storming? were not his prayers like strokes of a warlike engine, to make a breach in heaven, for his sister to enter at? Sweet Jesus! you that suffer this violence, are yourself the cause of it ; the good prelate breathes nothing but what you have inspired him ; so sweet are you in your mercies, so faithful in your promises, and so powerful in your divine wonders. Thus far St. Bernard. But I cannot let pass in silence one very remarkable passage,* which happened to these two great servants of God. St. Malachy had passionately desired to die at Clarvallis, in the hands of the devout St. Bernard ; and this, on the day immediately before All Souls' Day : and it pleased God to grant him his request. It fell out, then, that while St. Bernard was saying Mass for him, in the middle of Mass it was revealed to him, that St. Malachy was already glorious in heaven ; whether he had gone straight thither out of this world, or whether

* *i.e.* Event.

that part of St. Bernard's Mass had freed him out of Purgatory, is uncertain : but St. Bernard hereupon changed his note ; for having began a Requiem, he went on with the Mass of a bishop and confessor, to the great astonishment of all the standers-by. Oh, it is good to have such devout Masses said presently after one's death ! it is good to die in so good hands, as will not quit you till they have conducted you to the choir of Angels!

St. Thomas of Aquin, that great champion of Purgatory, gave God particular thanks at his death, for not only delivering a soul out of Purgatory, at the instance of his prayers, but also permitting the same soul to be the messenger of so good news.

Durand* argues the case thus : Sure, Christian charity has more power with Almighty God than a mere natural friendship can have with the civil magistrate ; now, it has been often seen, that a condemned person has been quit, at the earnest entreaty, or voluntary satisfaction, of their friends. Stories are full of such courteous civilities. How can we then make any question, but that God will as easily be moved to release holy souls out of Purgatory, at the sweet importunity of their friends' tears, prayers, and sufferings here upon earth? It was a laudable custom in some countries, that if a chaste virgin should present herself at the place of execution, to beg a felon for her husband, her request was granted, and the poor criminal was with great joy instantly conveyed from the gallows to a nuptial feast. This custom, though now out of date, may yet serve to tell us, that

* In 4, d. 45.

Almighty God will not deny to set a soul free from the punishment of all its misdemeanours, if we beg it earnestly at the hands of His infinite mercy.

And now, we are come down to the fifteenth age; where the Fathers of the Council of Florence, both Greeks and Latins, with one consent, declare the same faith, and constant practice of the Church, thus handed down to them from age to age, since Christ and His Apostles' time, as we have seen: viz. that the souls in Purgatory, are not only relieved, but translated into heaven, by the prayers, sacrifices, alms, and other charitable works, which are offered up for them according to the custom of the Catholic Church. Nor did their posterity degenerate, or vary the least, from this received doctrine, until Luther's time; when the holy Council of Trent thought fit again to lay down the sound doctrine of the Church, in opposition to all our late sectaries. And I wish all Catholics were but as forward to lend their helping hands to lift souls out of Purgatory, as they are to believe they have the power to do it: and that we had not often more reason than the Roman Emperor to pronounce the day lost; since we let so many days pass over our heads, and so many fair occasions slip out of our hands, without easing, or releasing, any souls out of Purgatory, when we might do it with so much ease.

THE SIXTH SURVEY.

OF TWELVE EXCELLENT MEANS TO PREVENT PURGA-
TORY, OR SO TO PROVIDE FOR OURSELVES, AS NOT
TO MAKE ANY LONG STAY THERE.

BEHOLD the most important point of all others, the
secret of secrets, and the true knack of all state
affairs in this world.   They talk of certain waters,
which have so strange a power to dull the edge of
fire, that if one wash his hands with them, he can
receive no prejudice, though he should thrust them
afterwards into the fire, or into boiling lead.   The preservatives I am here to treat of, are of a higher nature ;
they do not curb the restless activity of this our sublunary fire, which is bent only against dull bodies ; but
they arm us against the raging fire of Purgatory, which
God has prepared to torment our very souls in the
other world.

§ 1.—*The first, Perfect Contrition.*

One of the surest means to avoid Purgatory, is to
die with tears in our eyes, and true contrition in our
hearts.   For divines * teach that our contrition may
be so great, as to wash away all those spots of sin
which Purgatory fire was otherwise to have worn off.
And therefore, as I take it to be a great piece of folly
to defer the exercise of so precious an act unto the
hour of our death ; so I esteem it one of the most

* St. Thomas, *Suppl.* q. 5, a. 3.

solid devotions of all others, to accustom ourselves
to it all our lifetime: that, by daily frequenting such
acts, we may at length get such a habit and facility
in them, as, with God's grace, to have them at our call
when we come to die. All must not look for the
same privilege which the good thief had at the last
gasp. It was but little that he said; but he spoke it
with so cordial an accent, that he deserved to hear
those comfortable words of our Blessed Saviour ·
"This day thou shalt be with Me in Paradise;"
and soon found them verified by a present fruition
of the beatifical vision. Almighty God is pleased
sometimes to make so forcible an entry into the
heart of man, and to set it so desperately on fire
with His divine love, that there is no remedy but to
die between the arms of love and grief; and thrice
happy are those souls that lose their lives in this
divine encounter, and die in the most loving flames of
ardent charity; they are sure never to feel the murdering flames of Purgatory. Such was the death of our
Blessed Lady, St. John the Evangelist, and infinite
others, who have been straight carried into heaven
out of this world on the wings of love or contrition ;
so that a heart that is well seasoned with contrition,
or steeped in a bath of salt tears, is like the heart
of Prince Germanicus,* which being washed over with
a certain precious liquor, could not be consumed by
the fire which turned all the rest of his body to ashes.

This is what they call a good *Peccavi;* but it must
be a good one indeed: for it is not every ordinary and
trivial kind of sorrow which can work such wonders.

* Tacitus. *Ann.*

M

Those that have been long used to actuate themselves in those generous acts of contrition, may be full of confidence that the mercy of God will not fail them at the hour of their death; and that their good Angels will be then ready, when it most imports, to inspire them with all the best motives of true contrition : since they have gone all along with them, still furnishing them with such good thoughts, and so much good success, that their hearts have been a thousand times broken with a lively, a loving, and cordial contrition and repentance for their sins. And, certainly, they that die, either in the fire of so ardent a love or in the water of so piercing a grief, need not fear the fire of Purgatory; for that fire, says St. Bonaventure, was not made for them. So that, methinks, this charity may be fitly compared to the Seraphim at the gates of Paradise, brandishing his flaming sword, which Tertullian * calls the porter of Paradise; grief is the edge, love the fire, wherewith it is inflamed; and he that has this flaming sword, has heaven's gates at command, and goes straight thither when he leaves the world.

§ 2.—*The second, to die in Religion.*

Another safe way to escape Purgatory, is to live and die in a good religious Order, and at his death to renew and ratify his religious vows. To prove this,† I first call St. Bernard to witness, who doubts not to assure us that there is a ready, if not an uninterrupted passage, into heaven out of a religious cell. ˙ Next, I

* Romphæa janitrix Paradisi.
† *Ad Fratres de Monte Dei: à cella in cælum,* &c.

appeal to those holy and learned Doctors who give it for a certain sign of predestination to die in religion; because Christ has in a manner sworn, in His holy Gospel,* to give a hundred-fold and life everlasting to all those that shall leave father, mother, and other worldly concernments for His sake. From whence it is that Holy Church permits the superiors of divers religious Orders, to make this solemn promise at the profession of their novices, for they have no sooner made their vows of poverty, &c., but the Superior answers, "And I, child, do promise thee Paradise and eternal life."

3. Many Popes have granted a Plenary Indulgence,† in form of a Jubilee, to all religious persons, that either by word of mouth, or in their hearts, call upon the sacred names of Jesus and Mary, at the hour of their death. And what religious person is there that does it not, either when he dies or not long before, not only once, but a thousand times?

To say nothing, that many are of opinion that they gain this Indulgence at the hour of their death, whether they pronounce the words or no.‡ For, as other Indulgences are gained by visiting certain churches, saying certain prayers, giving alms, or exercising such other acts of virtue, the Supreme Pastor of the Church thought no act more worthy of a Jubilee than to die in a religious Order, in the actual profession of voluntary poverty, chastity, and obedience; with final perseverance in the austerity of a religious life, and a patient acceptance of our death, as from the

---

* Plat. *De Bono stat. Relig.*

† Sixt. Greg. xiii. Greg. xiv.   ‡ Jul. ii. Bull.

M 2

holy hand of God.   Let us, then, suppose a good
religious man to come to die; and, besides the
common benefit of the sacraments, and other hol
rites of the Catholic Church, let him gain this
Plenary Indulgence, which the Popes grant as freely
and with as much assurance as any other; have we
not all the reason in the world to hope that he goes
immediately into heaven, or, at most, does but make
a swift passage through Purgatory; or, rather, as we
read of many in the Ecclesiastical History, takes it in
his way, to have the company of some of his friends
there, whom he has the privilege to lead away with
him in triumph into heaven?

4. Who can better deserve to go directly into
heaven than they whose lives are a continual Purgatory?   They go in rough hair-shirts, pine themselves
with rigorous fasts, tear off their flesh with cruel disciplines, drink up their own tears, live on nothing but
mortifications and perpetual hardships, and thus
abundantly satisfy for all the sins they have committed, and for those they never dreamt of, but had
rather die a thousand times than commit.   They that
have no will but that of their Superior, they that
breathe nothing but holy sighs, and burn with ardent
charity, how can they burn in Purgatory fire? ·

5. Divines furnish me with another pregnant proof,
and it is this.   It is certain, say they, that a solemn
profession in religion brings with it a Plenary Indulgence or remission of all their sins, not only because it
is a second baptism, or a lingering kind of martyrdom,
which is not completed in a few moments, as other
martyrdoms are, but also, because in the opinion of

the Angelical Doctor,* it is so sublime and eminent an act, as surpasses all other acts in this life; so that if Daniel (says he) could say, that by giving a little alms we may blot out our sins, what may we not say of this supereminent act of liberality, by which a man gives unto God all his goods and present possessions, with all his fair hopes of improving them, his body, his life, his honour, his will, his soul; with a million of worlds, if he had them in his power? The same holy Doctor says elsewhere, that a man who sacrifices his will unto God, the most noble portion of his soul, and makes it to become His eternal slave, gives God full satisfaction for all his misdemeanours : since a mere creature cannot present Him with a more noble gift, than to make Him an entire holocaust of that which is dearest unto him in this world; which is, his will, and the absolute sovereignty over himself and all his concerns. Others† go yet further, and assure us that as often as a good religious man renews this his profession he makes a new purchase of the same favour, and obtains an entire pardon of all the pain due to his sins; and that these, and the like privileges, are not tied only to solemn vows, but are common to all vows that make up the substance of a religious man, of what Order soever in God's Church. And they say withal, that these favours are not in the nature of Indulgences granted by His Holiness, but are inseparably annexed unto the vows themselves; which are so generous, and so precious acts in the sight of God, that they move His goodness to blot out the

---

* 2. 2. 4. ult. a. 3.
† *Suarez, Verb. Religio,* n. 27, &c.

remembrance of their sins, and to cancel a great part, if not all, the pain which was due for them.

Now, put all this together; and it will necessarily follow that since the Pope, on the one side, grants a Jubilee unto all religious at the hour of their death, and since they have it in their power, on the other side, to renew their vows before they die, by which act they may fully satisfy for all their sins; there cannot be a greater assurance of going directly into heaven than theirs, who have, as I told you, this double security of a general pardon : that so, one way or other, they can scarce fail to obtain it.

What shall I say now of their perfect resignation unto the will of God; their invincible patience, their love of God, their virginal purity, their exact and punctual obedience, with a million of other divine acts of virtue, which are so incident and connatural to a religious vocation? all of which, no doubt, stand ready to assist them at the last hour, and to show them heaven's gates open and ready to receive them; and, howsoever, to assure them that their stay cannot be long in Purgatory, since they leave behind them so many of their own Order, who will be sure to ply them with Masses, Indulgences, and other charitable works, for their speedy deliverance.

§ 3.—*The third, to be an Apostolical Preacher.*

A third means to redeem Purgatory is be a zealous and apostolical preacher. For, as this is a life of eminent perfection and incredible merit, so is it extreme painful, and may well pass for a Purgatory in this life. But observe, that I speak of an apostolical preacher, or of one that is full of divine fire, or a holy zeal for the good of souls. I mean not those that preach themselves, those that desire to be admired and adored for oracles, those that profane the Word of God with their vain glosses, idle applications, and affected eloquence, seeking nothing more than worldly applause, and really destroying by their life and conversation all they build up in the pulpit. St. Paul compares such vain preachers to cracked trumpets, and broken bells, which make a noise indeed, but are altogether useless. They send others to heaven, said St. Xaverius, and go, God knows whither, themselves. St. Gregory likens them to the waters of baptism, which entitles children to the kingdom of heaven, and is itself conveyed into some noisome sink, and there turns to corruption. I speak, then, of a preacher who is a man of God; one that does what he says, and says what he does; one that aims at nothing but the salvation of souls, preaches to a few or to many, in cities or villages, princes' courts, or poor hospitals, with the same fervour of spirit. One that rends their hearts asunder, and draws floods of tears from their eyes; one that preaches like another St. Paul, and draws his sermons out of the Pentateuch of the five Wounds of his Redeemer; one that, after he has done all he can, believes he is an unprofitable servant, unworthy to open his mouth, or to tread upon the earth. Such a one, in my opinion, if he dies in the exercise of his holy function, either goes not at all to Purgatory, or stays not there. This was the case of

one Cherubim,* a famous preacher of the Order of
St. Francis ; who before he died had the comfort to
see St. Hierome, whom he had chosen for his peculiar
patron, and with him three thousand souls, all saved
by his means, who assured him that they were sent
expressly by Almighty God to carry him into heaven, and
so to requite him for showing them the way thither in
his zealous sermons.   Not unlike unto this, is that
story which I touched elsewhere, out of Cardinal
Baronius.   He tells us that St. Boniface† saw a holy
abbot at his death, surrounded with devils, and much
terrified to see them so insolent as to cry out, his soul
was theirs : when, behold ! his good Angel appears at
the head of a white troop of blessed souls ; who, after
a solemn profession that they had all been saved by
him, gave him the comfort to understand, they had
brought an express commission to convey him instantly
into heaven.   But you long now to have me paint
you out such a preacher : for, though there be many
that sooth themselves up with a vain persuasion that
they are the men ; yet, if we sift a little narrowly into
them, we should possibly find so much vanity, so
much care of esteem, so many by-ends, and so
many other imperfections to steal into their sermons,
that we may safely say, there are but few apostolical
preachers indeed, and such as seek only God's cause
and the good of souls.

  Take an exact idea, from one that lived but in the
last age.   Father Gonzales Silveria, of the Society of
Jesus, scarce ever went up into the pulpit without a

* Hist. St. Fran. l. 7, c. 2, p. 3.
† Annal. Eccl. an. 716.

hair-shirt; and would say, a man must be well armed
who goes to fight against vice.   It was also very usual
with him to encounter Goliah with David's sling; to
take a bloody discipline, and so to mount up into
the pulpit, and there, like thunder, to carry all before
him.   He had, for the most part, but five books for
his library: to wit, his Breviary, the Bible, the Lives
of Saints, a crucifix, and the picture of our Blessed
Lady. In these five books he studied for his sermons :
and certainly, the thunderbolts of his admirable
eloquence were framed in the Heart of his Crucified
Lord, the best furnace of divine love; the sweet
flowers of his rhetoric were steeped in the milk of the
Virgin ; his tropes and figures, and the whole variety of
his sermons, were borrowed out of the Word of God,
and the admirable lives of His Saints ; and lastly, the
religious and devout performance of his daily task of
divine office, and holy Mass, gave fire to his discourses,
wherewith he did not only heat, but inflame the hearts
of his auditors.   He would preach you twice or thrice
a day, and do it the more willingly in the meanest
places and to the poorest people. His common lodging
was the hospital, where he contented himself with a
spare diet and gross fare ; he was never observed to
be over-nice and coy of his sermons, nor required
he much time, to make them with applause. The
only thing he had before his eyes was the glory of
God and the help of souls; and his life preached
more than his tongue : for he really acted more in his
own person than he taught others.   As for his
manner of preaching, it was rather powerful than
charming; fitter to break their hearts, than please

their ears. Such was his fervour, that he poured his whole heart, and his whole zeal, out of his mouth; and he would be so transported with this zeal as not to take notice of anything else. Once, as he was preaching, he struck his hand upon a sharp nail which stuck out in the pulpit, and made it bleed so extremely, that the whole auditory took notice of it, and some of the devout women courteously offered their handkerchiefs to bind up the wound and stop the bleeding: and all this while the good man neither saw handkerchief, nor nail, nor blood, nor took the least notice of anything till after his sermon; when, the wound being grown cold, he was heard to wonder how the blood came there, and to complain that his hand put him to some pain. Another time, preaching in the Queen of Portugal's chapel, he had put himself into such a heat that, his mouth being clammed up, he could scarce get out his words; when the Queen, perceiving it, called for an ewer of water, which was instantly brought, and presented by the young Princess; but the man of God was so rapt in his devout thoughts, that he saw neither the ewer nor the Princess, nor the Queen; so that they were forced to pull him by the sleeve, that the Princess Royal might not stand thus waiting on him with the ewer in her hand; and then the Queen herself prayed him to make use of the water to cool and refresh his dry mouth. With much ado, the good Father came to himself; and, rising up, made a low obeisance to the Queen and Princess, thanked them for their care, excused himself for being so uncivil as not to mind them; but for all this would not take a drop of water, but went on with his sermon, to the great wonder and edification of all the standers-by. This, this is to preach like a man full of God's Spirit, like one that has his heart so transported with zeal, and his eyes so bent upon moving his auditors, that he can see nothing else. And would you have such a fiery man as this be condemned to Purgatory; one that has so much charity for others that he forgets himself, and distils out his life into blood, sweat, and tears, and is consumed in the fire of charity, which is the sweet purgatory of the servants of God?

§ 4.—*The fourth, to Serve the Infected.*

Those that charitably expose themselves to serve the infected, and so come to get the plague, and to die in the service, freely giving away their lives to save others, may have a great confidence that they have served out, if not all, at least the greatest part of their Purgatory. For, since an act of contrition or of perfect charity has power to make a soul instantly fit for heaven, as it falls out in martyrdom ; why may we not hope that the same privilege follows these charitable souls we speak of, who, though they die not by the hands of a bloody executioner, yet are cut off by a martyrdom of incomparable charity? Christ our Saviour said, that the greatest charity that a man could have in this life, was to give his life for his friends: where, by the way, St. Bernard notes, that His charity must needs be greater than the greatest, since He gave His divine life, not only for His friends, but even for His enemies. What shall we then think

of their charity, who voluntarily sacrifice their lives for
infected persons, whether friends or enemies, acquaintance or no acquaintance, rich or poor; and do it
generously, dying a thousand deaths for fear, danger,
and pain, before they come to die in good earnest?
Does not the Church list them amongst other Saints
in the Roman Martyrology? Does she not keep
their feast, and make an honourable commemoration
of their glorious death, on the 28th day of February?
Does she not withal tell us, that the faithful devout
people were accustomed to honour them as martyrs?
Would you, then, have these kind of martyrs, who die in
the fire of charity, go to Purgatory? To what purpose?
To metamorphose it into heaven? For if a maiden,
who is violently dragged away to some vile place,
which is a kind of hell, where massacre is made of immortal souls, in the opinion of St. Ambrose, changes it
into a kind of heaven, what can we think of those
charitable souls, but that, if they were conveyed into
the suffering Church, they would suddenly change
it into a Church triumphant? Hear a comfortable
story to this purpose. One Damian, of the holy
Order of St. Francis,* had devoted himself to serve
those that lay sick of the plague, with a burning
desire to give them all the comfort he could, by his
charitable visits. St. Francis met him one day, and
said: My son, didst thou but know what a crown in
heaven is prepared for thee, in reward of this charity
of thine, thou wouldst be out of thyself for mere joy;
go on, in God's name, for it will not be long before
thou art translated into heaven, to eternal glory. The

* *Annal. St. Fran.*

good friar continued the employment; till, one day, being in fervent prayer, he rendered up his happy soul into the hands of his Creator. Can you now believe that a man that sacrifices a good part of his life on the altar of the highest charity, which is in the world next unto martyrdom itself, one that loses his own life to make others live, and dies in the flames of a devout prayer; that this man, I say, goes to Purgatory? or, rather, do you not believe that heaven stoops to take him up, and to crown him with immortal glory?

Eusebius* takes a pleasure to relate the high esteem they had of those good priests, deacons, and secular persons, who thus exposed themselves to the plague, and sometimes were seen to tumble into the same graves where they had newly laid others. The fiery furnace, says St. Chrysostom,† was so astonished to see those three innocent creatures there, that it durst not touch them, but vented all its fury against the cords and fetters which bound them. Let us, then, suppose these holy souls to be cast into the furnace of Purgatory, who chose rather to forsake their lives than to forsake poor infected and forlorn creatures; can we imagine anything less, than that those subterraneous flames should yield, and with reverence submit unto the flames of heaven, which have already seized on those holy souls? and that they should say with Ecclesiasticus: "Thou hast delivered me, according to the multitude of Thy mercy . . . from the oppression of the flame which surrounded me, and

* Lib. i. c. 20.
† *Hom. de tribus pueris.*

in the midst of the fire I was not burnt."* What? shall purity have the power to resist fire, so that many chaste virgins have received no harm by it, and shall not charity in its perfection be as good a preservative against the fire of Purgatory?

§ 5.—*The fifth, a Tender Devotion to the Blessed Virgin.*

I cannot be persuaded that a soul, truly devoted to the honour and service of the Mother of God, can be long detained in Purgatory, if she go thither at all. For how should this be? Does our Blessed Lady want power? she that can do all things, says St. Anselm; or charity? she that has no feelings but of charity; she that has a heart so tender, that though you suppose a heart to be made up of all the mothers' hearts in the world, it could not be more tender than hers, which is all sweetness and tenderness. St. Bridget† had a son, who lived not so good a life as to look for heaven without passing through Purgatory. This great servant of God, who was not without the emotion of a loving mother, casts about how to save the poor youth, who was grown careless enough of himself. She resolves, therefore, to offer him up to the Blessed Virgin, and to trust her entirely with his salvation. She undertakes the trust, and carries it on so happily that, in fine, she saves him, and at the hour of death takes up his soul into heaven. This she did, by first working him to a perfect act of contrition,

* Ecclus. li. 4, 6.
† Osor. in S. Brig. Rev.

which imped his wings for heaven; and then cutting off the thread of his life, which should have held out one day longer: so that the devil, finding himself thus cozened, made his complaint to God, the just Judge· of the world; who returned this answer: "Know, that My Mother is Lady and Queen of Heaven, and therefore has liberty to place there whom she pleases; and what she does in this kind is well done, and pleasing in My sight." There is a world of examples of the like favours graciously showered down from the Mother of Mercy, who has often taken the pains to conduct her good children and faithful servants into heaven. And when it stands not with God's justice but that a soul must go into Purgatory, what does she not to help it out? as well by her ·own powerful intercession, which she will be sure to interpose, as far as it may stand with the just degrees of heaven; as by the prayers of her devout servants, into whose hearts she inspires a thousand good thoughts of tenderness for their souls, who were particularly devoted to her. How many divine consolations and refreshments does she send them by their good Angels? And, since it is certain that she goes sometimes to visit them on their death-beds, why may we not piously imagine that she gives them the like comfortable visits, when they lie tied to their beds of fire in cruel torments? The lioness and the tigress, though never so fierce by nature, will leap into the fire to save their young ones, or perish there. God forbid we should make any comparison between the Blessed Virgin, Mother of the Lion of Juda, and these wild beasts; and yet, since we

must allow so much tenderness to such cruel and
savage mothers, we may not doubt but that the
Mother of Mercy, seeing her beloved children in
the fire of Purgatory, will fly thither to fetch them
out.

The devout and learned Richard of St. Victor,*
commenting upon these words of the psalmist, "He
shall not be confounded, when he shall speak to his
enemies in the gate:" tells us, that this gate is the
Blessed Virgin; to appear at the gate, is to die, and
to be cited to particular judgment, where no body,
says he, is ever confounded that finds but this gate
favourably open; and to whom should the Mother of
God be favourable, but unto those that were constant
in her service? and from what confusion does she
deliver them, but from the dreadful fire of hell and
Purgatory? O God! what assurance have we, when
the Queen of Heaven is pleased to plead for us, and
to procure us a favourable sentence; and since it is
her well beloved Son that is to be our Judge, who
denies her nothing, what may we not hope for?
When St. John Damascene had lost his hand, he
begged it again of the Queen of Heaven,† and his
suit was instantly granted, so sure it is, that she
denies nothing to her dear children; what favours
then may not a devout soul look for at her hands,
when it departs out of this world?‡ If Mary hold
thee by the hand, fear not falling, cries St. Bernard;§

* Psalm cxxvi; Rich. c. 39 *in Cant.*
† Sur. in ejus vita : Metaphrast.
‡ Bern. he. i. sup. mistes est.
§ "Maria tenente non corruis," &c.

for, if she be propitious, thou art sure to have thy
share in the kingdom of heaven. Now, to whom will
she be propitious, if not to those that, while they
lived, breathed nothing but her love and service; and
when should she show herself more our friend, than
when we are threatened with Purgatory fire, which
burns so dreadfully?

The holy Abbot Guericus*˙ had reason to wish
rather to be lodged in the bosom of the Blessed
Virgin, than in Abraham's bosom. Oh, it is no small
security, to be under her protection, though it were
to throw it into Purgatory? God the Father? How?
but under her feet: for who should fetch a soul thence,
Out of the hands of His beloved daughter? Who
then? God the Son? How, from His beloved
Mother? Who then? God the Holy Ghost? What,
from His dearest Spouse? Who then? St. Michael
with his sword and buckler? That were pretty, that
a creature should attempt what the Blessed Trinity
forbears out of love to the Mother of God. Who
then? The devil? What! the serpent, whose head she
crushed under her feet, or any of his fellows, who
tremble at the very sound of her name? No; there
is not the creature dare meddle with a soul that is
once sheltered under the royal mantle of her protection. So true it is, that one of the best preservatives against Purgatory, is to be very devout to the
Blessed Virgin, Mother of God.

But it must be more than an ordinary devotion˙
as, to make a vow of chastity in her honour; to devote
oneself entirely to her; to do her some signal piece

* *Serm.* i. *De Assump.*

N

of service; to call often upon her, and with a filial
confidence; to build a goodly chapel, or some house
where she may be served to the world's end; to give
liberal and frequent alms for her sake; to compose
some excellent work in her praise, and so to draw
many others to her service : again, to maintain poor
scholars, in a way to be preachers or religious men,
with this obligation, that they shall make it their
study, all their lives, to preach her greatness, to
promote her service, and to draw all the world after
her. To make her a present of Masses, Communions,
fasts, disciplines, and other mortifications ; but, above
all, to imitate her glorious virtues, and to regulate our
lives accordingly. If you do these, and the like
things, and do them with a good heart, you need not
fear Purgatory will do you any great harm. She will
obtain for you such a measure of true contrition, such
a proportion of love and conformity to God's will, so
much patience in your last sickness, such holy and
ardent desires to serve God, such profound humility,
in a word, such heroic acts of virtue, as to blot out of
your soul what Purgatory was to have done, and put
you in a present capacity to go directly into heaven :
and if an extraordinary pass should be necessary, who
can better procure it for you, than the Lady of the
House, the Mother of the Judge, the Empress of
Paradise, and Princess of the Universe ?

§ 6.—*The sixth, an Humble Patience.*

You, that suffer great miseries in this world, may comfort yourselves with such precious sufferings : for, so* you be faithful to God ; so you voluntarily embrace what God sends, in spite of impatience; so you sub-mit to the laws of His sweet rigour, which chastises you ; so you freely offer all your little all to this great Lord of all, the great All of the whole universe ; so, from time to time you be still letting fall some good word, to testify that your soul and your body play not at the same game, move not upon the same centre, but that while the one is oppressed and cries out, the other secretly praises the paternal goodness of Almighty God ; so that you do all this, you may be confident there will be little or no Pur-gatory for you; having a Purgatory in this world, there is no reason you should have another hereafter.

I learn this secret of St. Gregory,† who admires a poor paralytic that lay rotting on a straw bed, where he had lived so all his life ; or, rather, where he had died so all his : life his life being nothing else but a mere concatenation of hourly deaths. Servulus was the name of this poor wretch, who at his death was comforted with angelical music, and carried away by Angels to sing his own part in heaven for all eternity. One of those that were present told St. Gregory, that at the hour of his happy departure out of this life, so sweet a smell was spread all over

i.e. So that, or, if only.
† Hom. 15 *in Evang.*

N 2

the little room where he lay, that he never felt the like ; and that this continued, and was perceived by all the standers-by, until his holy body was laid in his grave, and the service ended. But you will say : everybody cannot be so holy as this good man. Certainly they may, by the grace of God ; for St. Gregory observes but four things in him, which you may command as well as he. First, he often read the holy Scriptures, to comfort his heart in his sufferings. Secondly, he gave a part of the alms he received of good people, unto other needy persons, and lodged poor pilgrims in his poor cottage. Thirdly, holy aspirations and devout breathings were often heard to proceed from him, which were like so many fiery darts shot into the Heart of God, and bringing thence the sweet air of Paradise to refresh his soul, which by such amorous entertainments found less trouble in her afflictions. Fourthly, he was sensible enough of his pain, and would complain of it sometimes ; I say complain : do you think Saints have bodies of steel ? but, between one complaint and another, he would be often thus sweetly interposing : O my God, I desire Thy will may be fulfilled in all things, and nothing else but Thy will ! I am willing that Thou handle this my body, and all that belongs to me, according to Thy divine pleasure, both in time and eternity.

Now tell me, dear reader : canst thou not do all this, as well as this poor paralytic, who lived for no other end but to be dying a lingering death all the days of his miserable and yet thrice happy life ? Will you have a soul so holy, and so pliable to God's

will, be thrown into Purgatory fire? Sure, said
St. Austin, if He meant to damn us in the other
world, He would not damn us in this, to a hell of
most loathsome and intolerable diseases. And I
may say the like here; that if God meant to punish
His servants in Purgatory after this life, He would
not punish them here in a Purgatory of miseries.
His goodness is not wont to punish the same fault
twice. Go into hell and Purgatory, while you live,*
cried St. Bernard; and you will be sure not to go
thither after your death: for it is not reasonable that
you should have two purgatories, or hells. Alas!
no; and this is the cause why God, to save His
friends from those horrible torments of Purgatory fire,
sends them good store of crosses and afflictions in
this world, which are nothing so painful; and yet are
highly meritorious in His sight, whereas the other
are but pure sufferings. Hear St. Chrysostom : † The
tongue that praises God in the midst of afflictions
is not inferior to the tongues of martyrs, and likely
they may have both the same reward. If a man
praise God, and give Him thanks in his sufferings,
it is reputed as a kind of martyrdom; and would
you have a martyr go to Purgatory, he that finds
heaven open, and ready to receive him? For, as
Emissenus says very well, the heavens are not only
open to St. Stephen, but unto all martyrs, and
unto all that suffer and die with the name of Jesus
in their mouths, constancy in their hearts, and fidelity
in their souls. The works of patience, according to

* *In illud: Descendant in infernum viventes.*
† Hom. viii. in c. 3, *Ad Colon.*

St. James, are perfect;* and that which is perfect,
owes nothing to Purgatory; nor can Purgatory refine
that which is already perfect, no more than our fire
can refine gold of twenty-four carats, that is so pure
as not to have the least mixture of dross or impurity.

§ 7.—*The seventh, Devotion for the Souls in Purgatory.*

Shall I deal candidly with you? one of my chief
motives of publishing this treatise was to persuade you
this truth, that one of the best means to prevent Purgatory, is to have a great tenderness and a particular
care to comfort the souls there; to spare nothing that
can further their deliverance; in a word, to make
yourself a general agent for this suffering Church, to
solicit for their eternal rest. Take now the proofs of
this assertion, and the whole strength of my discourse.

1. Christ said, in plain terms: "With what measure
you mete, it shall be measured to you again;"† that
is, you shall be dealt withal in the same manner as
you deal with others. So that, if you have beat your
brains, and employed all your endeavours to help the
souls in Purgatory, and have really delivered some
before their time, it is but reason that this your charity
should be requited with a like return, and with a
hundred-fold besides; and heaven at the end of it.
Methinks, your case is not unlike to that of the
prudent Abigail. King David was so highly incensed
against the ungrateful Nabal,‡ that he swore to pursue

* St. James i. 4.
† St. Matt. vii. 2.   ‡ 1 Kings xxv.

him and his whole family with fire and sword, and to turn all into ashes. For all this, Abigail ventured to meet him with ·a present, and did it with so good a grace, that she soon made up the breach, and saved all. For David, after some little dispute with his anger, grew calmer, forgave all, and so sent her away joyfully in peace. The application is easy. It is true, you have played the ungrateful Nabal ; you have offended God, so far as to provoke His high displeasure,- so that He may seem to deal favourably with you, if He sends you into Purgatory; but you have withal played Abigail's part, in sending Him as many grateful presents as you have breathed out fervent prayers for the souls in Purgatory ; and with these you have made your peace, so that you may look to be dismissed in peace into the kingdom of heaven.

2. Take a second reason, of St. Peter; who exhorts us above all things to have charity for one another, because " charity covereth a multitude of sins." * For, since it is the greatest charity in the world to help poor souls out of Purgatory, as I proved at large in the Third Survey, those that devote themselves wholly to this service may be confident so to cover their sms, as to put them out of the reach of Purgatory fire. When Gibellin had straightly besieged Guelph, Duke of Bavaria, and forced him to surrender his town upon such hard terms,† as that the women only were permitted to secure themselves, and to take away with them what they could carry upon their backs ; but as for the men, they were to remain at mercy, exposed to the fury· of the fire and sword :—the good women,

* 1 St. Peter iv. 8.   † Parud. l. 2. c. 70.

laying their heads together, found out this strange
expedient to save their husbands, as well as themselves; for every one taking her husband upon her
back, and what else she was able to carry about her,
they marched out of the town.   Never was man so
struck with astonishment as Gibellin was at this sight;
and, though he might have disputed their passage, as
not consisting with the true meaning of the articles,
yet was he so taken with so rare a stratagem, and
strange example of a true conjugal love, that he suffered them all to pass freely, to the admiration of the
whole world.   And, surely, we may hence conclude,
that all those who have so much love for the poor
souls in Purgatory as to carry them, as it were, upon
their backs, out of their miserable thraldom, will find
heaven-gates open, and all the blessed spirits ready
to receive them with acclamations of joy, for so sweet
an excess of charity.

3. It is not possible, that they who have been thus
ransomed out of Purgatory by the ardent zeal of their
friends here, should not hold themselves obliged to
restitution; to return, I say, the like charity to the
souls of their benefactors, when they leave the world.
How can those happy souls, that swim in the ocean
of overflowing charity, choose but employ all their
power and interest to make them so?   But sure I
need not go about to multiply reasons in a case so
clear of itself, so full of piety and heavenly fitness.
I will only mind you of what I told you elsewhere out
of Cajetan, how reasonable a thing it is, that all those
holy strays, or wandering suffrages, which are offered
up for such souls as are not in Purgatory, should be

applied unto them that had a particular affection and devotion to help souls out of that fiery dungeon; and this certainly will be a means to fetch them out quickly, if they ever come there.

§ 8.—*The eighth, to be a great Alms-giver.*

The eighth means to prevent Purgatory, is to be very liberal and tender-hearted to the poor. The Holy Ghost teaches us as much, in most emphatical and comfortable words; some whereof I have chosen to lay down before you, with a desire to imprint them in your hearts. "Blessed is he that understandeth concerning the needy and the poor; the Lord will deliver him in the evil day. The Lord preserve him and give him life, and make him blessed upon the earth: and deliver him not up to the will of his enemies. The Lord help him on his bed of sorrow."* These words need no gloss. For what is this evil day, but the day of particular judgment at the hour of death? since it is the great critical day, and the most considerable moment, upon which eternity depends. Now, he tells us, that God will deliver him this day; from what, I pray you, if not from eternal fire, and from the dreadful fire of Purgatory, according to the measure of his charity and liberality to the poor? He tells us again, that He will make him happy in this day; out of which I conclude, that he shall not go into Purgatory; for how can he be happy that day, if he lie in flames of fire? Call you this to deliver a man from evil, to plunge him over head and ears in a fiery

* Psalm xl. 1—4

gulf ? St. Chrysologus spoke with a grace when he said,* that charity will not suffer a great alms-giver to be laid in fire, but will appeal from the sentence, and move God to cancel His own decree ; and, in a word, will have him to be saved ; and all this, with so sweet a violence, says the same Saint, that God had rather alter His decree, than contristate mercy and charity when they plead with such power for a great alms-giver. Let us hear the Holy Ghost once more, I pray you. "Water quencheth a flaming fire, and alms resisteth sins; and God provideth for him that showeth favour : He remembereth him afterwards, and in the time of his fall he shall find a sure stay. . . Son, bow down thy ear cheerfully to the poor : be merciful to the fatherless as a father, and as a husband to their mother ; and thou shalt be as the obedient son of the Most High, and He will have mercy on thee, more than a mother." † O God, what sweet words are these ! When he is about to fall, he shall find a sure stay ; when he is ready to sink into Purgatory he shall be held up: he shall be strengthened, he shall be raised above the firmament, he shall be carried into Paradise. What! would a loving mother do less, if it were in her power? And since God has given us His word, that He will be more than a mother to such charitable souls, that is, have a greater tenderness and love for them, is it credible that He will suffer them to fall into Purgatory? or, if justice require some satisfaction there, is it not likely that all means will be used to remove them out of hand ? The Cæsars crowned themselves with laurel, as fancying it to be a sure protection

* Serm. 8.   † Ecclus. iii. iv.

against fire from heaven ; but I may safely say, that a merciful soul, all covered over with laurels, olive-branches, and refined gold of charity, cannot be struck with fire from heaven, and has as little reason to fear the fire of Purgatory.

It is better, said St. Chrysostom,* to give alms to the poor, than to work a miracle, or to raise a dead man; for in this you are beholding to God, but in that God is beholding to you. And therefore, since God is indebted to you, tell Him plainly you will be paid with no other coin but that of Paradise. If He thinks of sending you to Purgatory, tell Him you will be first paid what He is pleased to owe you; for He has promised you life everlasting : and, therefore, let Him first place you in Paradise, and you will have leisure there to talk of Purgatory. It was an answer worthy of eternal memory, that of the good Count Thibaud of Champagne. A poor gentleman fell at his feet, with tears in his eyes, saying : My lord, you are the father of the poor ; I have two daughters to marry, and have no way to compass it, having nothing in the world to give them ; those poor creatures are utterly lost, if you take not pity on them and me, your most humble servant, and therefore, I beseech your honour to have mercy on us. The two poor young women were all this time on their knees, as beautiful as the sun, their eyes humbly cast down upon the ground, and their faces covered with a modest and virginal blush ; when out steps a ruffian-like courtier, his name was Arrant, and rudely tells the poor gentleman, it was a pretty sight, indeed,

* Hom. 39 *ad Pop.*

to see him beg an alms with his sword by his side. Besides, he was to know that the Count was not for nothing surnamed the Bountiful; for he had given away so much, that he had no more left to bestow. " How ! " replied the Count, " that is not so ; I have yet something left, God be thanked, and enough too to bestow upon the good gentleman ; for I am willing to part with thee, and to yield up unto him all the interest I have taken in thee. " So, take him, friend," continued he, " and be sure you do not part with him till he has bestowed both your daughters." This he said; and it fell out so in good earnest: for the courtier was glad at his own charge to provide competent portions for the two poor young women, and all France admired, and highly extolled the Count, for his prudent carriage of the whole business. Can you find in your heart to condemn such a brave prince to Purgatory, after he has left many such charitable examples behind him? one, I say, that has given so much away in pious uses, that he has no more to give ; one that would willingly have sold himself, after all, to make an alms of the price to our Blessed Saviour, in the person of those poor innocent doves.

The Angel Raphael deserves credit, when he tells us, in expressive terms, that it is better to give alms than to lay up treasures of gold : because that is it which purgeth sin, and maketh us find mercy and life everlasting.* How does your heart feel, at this comfortable lesson? since charity has the power to purge sin, what need of another Purgatory? and

Tob. xii. 8, 9.

since she is so happy as to procure life everlasting,
have you not reason to hope she will, at your death,
set heaven's gate open, and lead you in thither, as it
were by the hand? When those dutiful children*
took their parents on their backs, to deliver them out
of the flames, which were furiously vomited out of
Etna, to the terror of all Sicily, which seemed to be
all on a light fire, they say, the flames, out of respect
to this natural affection, parted themselves, and made
a lane for the youths to pass through without harm,
that had so much love for their parents, whose age
and feebleness would have otherwise betrayed them to
utter destruction; and so all, for company, were
happily saved out of that furious purgatory. And
certainly, if your charity take you up, if your mercy
do but hide you in her bosom, when you shall pass
through Purgatory the fire will be so courteous as to
retire, and give way to your passage : they will set all
the gates open for you to get out when you please,
and bring you the keys of Paradise.

§ 9.—*The ninth, Angelical Purity.*

The ninth, and a very efficacious preservative
against Purgatory, is a special chastity, or virginal
purity. I cannot think that a pure and humble heart,
a soul that is newly divorced from a virginal body,
can ever be tied to purging flames. The diamond of
chastity has, I know not what, that makes it victorious
over flames; this Mount Libanus, as white as snow,
is never visited with fire from heaven; this virginal

* Val. Max.

laurel, which triumphs over the pleasures of this world, fears not the fury of any subterraneous flames; this St. John may be plunged into boiling oil without feeling the least smart; this royal salamander can live untouched in the midst of fire; this pure gold suffers no detriment in the crucible; this eagle cuts her way through the element of fire, and soars up to heaven without singeing her wings; these innocents sing merrily in the furnace of Babylon, as if they were in terrestrial Paradise. In earnest, there is no reason that persons, as chaste as Angels, who were invincible and untouched in the flames of concupiscence, which devour almost all the world; there is no reason, I say, that those who were proof against these subtle alluring flames, should not appear as good proof against these other cruel, devouring flames; or they should ever feel the smart of the one, that had so valiantly overcome the false flatteries of the other. St. John says, that virgins follow the Lamb wheresoever He goes; they are the ordinary courtiers of Jesus Christ, that have washed their robes in the Blood of the Lamb. And shall such clean, innocent souls need the help of Purgatory fire, to wash away their stains? St. Teresa, once seeing a canon in the Church, ready to be laid in his grave, and, another time, one of the Society, who was also laid upon the bier, ran instantly to kiss their dead corpses: and when all were astonished to see her, she told those whom it concerned, that she was very certain that those two reverend persons were virgins, and that their happy souls had for that cause taken flight into heaven, just as they parted with their bodies.

The Greek History* tells us, that when, in the heat of the tyrant's persecution, Nicomedia fell to the plunder of the rude soldiers, amongst others they took a young maiden; and having in vain laboured to make her sacrifice unto idols, they threatened her with a base and cruel alternative. She, on her part, begged leave to speak a word or two to Anthimus the bishop. To him she proposed this case of conscience, whether she might not rather choose to die, or to be accessory to her own death, than lose the precious pearl of her purity. The good Bishop made her so doubtful an answer, that she could not well determine what he meant. Hereupon she is hurried away instantly; when the following expedient came into her thoughts; seeing one of the plundering soldiers, she speaks thus to him: "Friend, I promise to teach thee a receipt that will make thee immortal; whereby thou shalt become the most valiant and famous man living; the secret is dear to me as my honour and my very life." He answers her, he was content, so she could but make her words good. "Sir, I have," says she, "a precious ointment, which is of so great virtue, that whosoever is anointed with it, can receive no harm. A thousand rude blows or desperate thrusts of a sword cannot do him the least hurt against his will." "How shall I believe this paradox," replies the soldier, "which you speak possibly only to amuse me, or rather to abuse me?" "Sure you will believe it," says she, "when you see it tried before your eyes." Away she goes, borrows a little oil of the next lamp she meets with, returns instantly, shuts the door, bares

* Cedren. *Annal.*

her neck, rubs it well over with this miraculous oil
that is to make people immortal; then casts herself
down on her knees, and bids the soldier sure to take
good aim, and strike boldly, and spare not; for he
should soon see a fair trial of this wonderful experi-
ment. With this she casts up her eyes smilingly
towards heaven, and begs of sweet Jesus, her beloved
Spouse, that the oil might have the effect she much
longed for, to preserve her pure. Meantime, the
soldier lifts up his sword, and with all his might levels
it at the neck of the innocent virgin; and in a trice
strikes off her head, which lay reeking in blood, a good
distance from the rest of her body. Never was man
so amazed and confounded as this soldier, to see himself thus fooled. But let us leave him to vent his
fury by himself, and fall to considering this prodigious
courage, this exceeding love of purity, this ingenious
stratagem of the young maiden; this innocent murder,
or harmless contrivance of her own death, in obedience to a particular instinct of the Holy Ghost, as we
may piously imagine; and, having taken a full view of
all these circumstances, let us see whether we have the
conscience to condemn the young lady to Purgatory
fire, who was so chaste as to choose rather to die than
part with her virginal integrity.

Which of you, said the Prophet Isaias,* can dwell
in devouring fire without burning? Answer; It is
chastity. Which of you can carry fire in his bosom,
or lie in the bosom of fire, without hurt, cried
Solomon?† Answer; It is chastity. Again; which
of you can walk upon firebrands or tread upon

* Isaias xxxiii. 14.   † Prov. vi. 27, 28.

glowing coals, as upon a bed of flowers? Answer; It is a virginal chastity. Witness St. Agnes, who lay smiling in the midst of a most cruel fire. Witness St. Thecla, who could walk as confidently upon hot burning coals, as if they had been roses. Witness St. Apollonia, who made nothing of leaping into a dreadful fire which was prepared for her. Witness a thousand other virgins, who were seen to triumph in flames of fire, as if they had been in the empyrean heaven.* You may remember the most chaste and incomparable virgin, Restituta, who, being condemned to be burnt alive, was for that purpose put into an old ship, full of pitch, brimstone, and fire, and thus exposed to the mercy of those merciless elements. She appeared in the midst of the sea, as in a floating fire, upon her knees; and there she breathed out her sweet soul into the hands of her heavenly Spouse, leaving her virginal body still entire, and without suffering the least detriment, by the smoke or by the fire. Now, it was the fire of divine love that gave her the mortal wound; no other fire durst touch or consume that virginal flesh, which was consecrated to her dear Saviour, by the fair hands of chastity. Go; cast me such a soul into Purgatory fire, and let it do its worst, and burn her if it can. No; fire will sooner melt a diamond, and all things that are the most impossible will sooner come to pass, than a pure and angelical virgin shall feel the smart of tormenting fire; which has the discretion, says St. Chrysostom,† to distinguish innocency from

---

* Mart. Rom. 17 May.
† Hom. *De tribus innocent.*

O

guilt, and to fly furiously upon the one, while with veneration and reverence it fawns upon the other.

§ 10.—*The tenth, a Profound Humility.*

It cannot enter into my head that a soul which is truly humble shall ever enter into this place of torments, much less be long detained there. They say there is a bird, that will be sure to save herself in all occasions of danger, by sinking down so low into the water, as to be out of all reach. The soul of a man that is truly humble sinks down so deep into the centre of her own nothing, that there is not the thing under heaven that can come near her, to annoy her: and if, by chance, a little Purgatory fire should be let down upon her, it would do by her as, they say, the fire which falls from heaven does by a piece of well disposed mould, which is so far from burning and destroying it, that it converts it into some precious stone. The great God of Heaven, who loves to crush the heads of ambitious persons, to lay them level with the ground, and to grind them to powder, takes pleasure to raise humble souls out of the dirt, to make them prime potentates of Paradise, and to sit among the princes of His heavenly kingdom. He that would be sure to find the glory of the Saints, said St. Dorotheus,* must seek it in the bosom of humility; for there, and only there, all true joy, content, and happiness are to be found. Paradise will sooner stoop down to Purgatory, than suffer an humble soul to lie burning in those merciless flames. Would you, says St. Chysostom,† pass quickly through the raging

---

* *Serm.* i.   † Hom. 38 *ad Pop.*

and tempestuous ocean? Be sure that humility be
your pilot. When St. Paul took himself for no better
than the dust of the common streets, then it was that
he was rapt up to the third heaven. True; and I
may be bold to tell you, that if you be but humble,
they will not easily make you stoop so low as Purgatory, but will rather lift you up above the wings of
Seraphim. The royal Prophet made it his prayer to
God to look down upon his humility, to consider his
labours, and to blot out all his sins, and make him as
innocent as an Angel, or a child of a year old. What
has an Angel or an infant to do in Purgatory?* Some
hold a man that is very humble, to be a kind of
martyr. Must martyrs be sent, like criminals, to
broil in Purgatory? No, no: says Climacus,† rejoice
not that you have the gift of miracles, like an Apostle,
or that you tread all the devils in hell under your feet;
it is a greater advantage to be humble, and to have
your names written in the golden book of humility.
Shall such as stand in competition with Apostles, be
sent into Purgatory? There are stones of so happy a
temper, that though they should lie a thousand years
in a hot furnace, they would not be the worse for it,
but become still more fair and beautiful. Behold the
true emblem of humility. Purgatory will be sooner
turned into Paradise, than do an humble soul the least
prejudice. Esther, whose very name carries humility,
was ready to die, when she saw the majesty of King
Assuerus; she humbled herself, and lay prostrate at his
feet; and what followed? They were so far from
putting her to death, according to the laws of the

* St. Doroth. *Serm.* 2 *De Humil.*   † *Grad.* 25.

kingdom, that they placed her in the Queen's throne, and made her one of the greatest princesses of her time. When God sees a soul that is humble in good earnest to lie prostrate at His feet, He has not the heart to condemn her to death, or to torments. " My friend," will He say, " mount up higher ; it is not your place to lie there, melting in Purgatory : mount up higher, and do it boldly ; for I love to raise those high that humble themselves low, and of the children of Abraham, who esteem themselves no better than a little dust, I make the stars of My firmament, and the Angels of My Paradise." It is a strange thing to see that poor Lazarus, humble and contemptible as he was, comes no sooner to die, but the Angels do him the honour to conduct him into Abraham's bosom. And the good thief, who had scarce any other virtue to plead for him, but a little humility, to confess himself a vile wretch, as he was, did scarce find himself in the other world, but he found himself in Paradise. So true it is, that God loves humility ; and that all the heavens stand open to entertain those that are truly humble.

§ 11.—*The eleventh, to Communicate well and often.*

I should never make an end, should I go about to bring in all the heroical virtues which are strong antidotes, and powerful preservatives, against the fire of Purgatory : and yet I cannot choose but vent a thought or two more, which, with the rest, I submit to your discreet judgment.

And first; I take those that communicate often, and do it well and worthily, to be pretty secure from feeling any great smart in Purgatory.   St. Ignatius· had reason to style the Holy Eucharist, the antidote of immortality.*

The Romans used to put a piece of silver in the dead man's mouth ; and verily believed, that by giving this for his passage, he should be conveyed safe to the Elysian fields.   This was a vain superstition; but you must give me leave to fancy, that when a good Christian dies, with his Saviour in his mouth, or in his heart, all Paradise lies open to receive him. "Open your gates, you princes of heaven; open your gates, for behold the King of Glory is ready to make His entrance ;"† in the triumphant chariot of virtues, sitting in a heart as white as ivory, which serves Him for His royal throne.   Roger, King of Sicily, ‡ having long laboured in vain to make himself master of the Island of Corfu, at length, tired out with so long a siege, fell upon this noble stratagem.   He makes as if a nobleman of the town were dead in his camp, who desired to be buried within their walls, with the rest of his ancestors.   He was accordingly laid upon the bier, and covered like a dead corpse ; a noble convoy was prepared to attend the hearse, with torches in their hands ; nothing was wanting to make up a complete funeral.   The town, mistrusting nothing, set open their gates to let them in ; but my counterfeit dead man was scarce got upon the drawbridge, ready to enter the town, when, behold ! he suddenly changes

* Epist. *ad Ephes.*
† Psalm xxiii. 7.   ‡ Hist. Neap. l. I. p. 2.

the whole scene; revives, and starts up with his sword in his hand, which was a sign for all his attendants to throw away their torches and to betake themselves to their weapons : and they managed them so well, that they first took the gate, and then the town, and the whole island; to the great terror and astonishment of their enemies, who found themselves gulled and surprised with so unexpected and so unusual a ceremony. A grave prelate terms the Holy Eucharist the incordiation of God;* as if he would have said that God, in this Holy Sacrament, is as it were incorporated into our hearts, and our hearts into God; so that God lying thus hidden within us, He that is Lord of the celestial Jerusalem, to which our hearts have laid so close and loving a siege, if we present Him to the blessed inhabitants, as dead for the love of us, they dare not but admit Him, and them also that carry Him, after this manner, in the very centre of their hearts and souls.

Upon occasion of a hot contest at Florence, about Savonarola, when some would have him an heretic, others not, there were two, amongst others, who took a strange resolution to put it to the trial of the fire : and he that could endure the flames better, was to be thought to have the better cause. The day agreed on being come, the fire prepared for the purpose, and all the world longing to see the success of this strange challenge, it was discovered that one of the parties had hid the Blessed Sacrament in his bosom; believing that the fire would not hurt him, while he carried so precious a treasure about him. What came of it, and

* Paris, *lib. de Euchar.*

what was the conclusion of the whole business, you may read at leisure in the history itself. I only bring this, to show the man's confidence in this powerful preservative; and then you may please to remember, how the Sacred Host has been sometimes seen to hang in the air, surrounded about with flames, and thus to have been miraculously preserved. I know, we are not always to look for miracles of this nature; and yet, methinks, we may be confident, that Purgatory fire will have nothing to do with a soul where Christ has been pleased to take up His constant lodging. Where the King is, there is the Court; where Christ is, says Sinesius,* there must needs be good fortune and victory; where God is, says St. Austin, there is Paradise. Nay: though you were in the deepest pit of Purgatory, God would not deny you entrance into heaven, who never refused to entertain Him in your heart; He never knocks at your door but you were still ready to receive Him: can you think He will be less courteous to you in the other world?

Besides all this, he that receives often and devoutly, receives withal such store of heavenly lights, such a tenderness of heart, such inflamed desires, so much innocency in his conversation, and so much purity of intention in all his actions; he is withal so transformed into God, upon whom he feeds and feasts himself continually: he is so identified with Him, and, to use the phrase of St. Denis and St. Bonaventure, is so straitly united with God, that, as St. Paul speaks of them that cleave to God, he becomes one spirit, and, as it were, one thing with God. This being so,

* Syn. *Epist.* iii.; Aug. *De Gen. ad litt.*

will you have this heart, which is but one thing with Christ, to be swallowed up in Purgatory, and so carry Christ thither? They say, Albertus Magnus held, and, whether he held it or no, I know many other worthy persons maintain, that one single thought of the most bitter Passion of our Blessed Saviour is so powerful, and so effectual,* that a man may gain sometimes more by it, than if he had fasted with bread and water, or disciplined himself every day till blood comes, or read over daily the whole Psalter. I mean not to examine now the truth of this assertion, according to the rigour of divinity: I only say that in some sense it may be true; and this makes very much for my present purpose. For there is not the thing in the world, that is a more lively representation of the Passion of Christ, than the Blessed Sacrament; which He left expressly as an eternal memorial of His Passion: commanding us to remember His death and bitter Passion, when we receive Him, and still acting in our hearts that sad tragedy, though without the effusion of His Blood; and imprinting in our souls the several passages of His most precious death. Of what merit, then, must a Holy Communion be; and a Communion which is often frequented, and continued to the hour of death? If such as these go to Purgatory, sure, there will be none free. St. Thomas tells us, the Blessed Sacrament is called a pledge of eternal life. "Now," says he, "we never use to deliver up our pledge, until we are possessed of the thing for which it was engaged; see then," saith he, "that you part not with the Body of Christ unto His Eternal Father,

---

* Granad. *De Orat. De Pont.* p. 4. *Medit.*

till He has received you into Paradise, for which it was given you as a most precious and secure pledge." Hence it is that St. Ambrose * styles it a parcel of eternal life; an essay or taste; a certain infallible assurance of enjoying it: and St. Cyprian† calls it an infusion of the divine essence; and St. Bonaventure, a wonderful deification, a metamorphosing of the heart, by which a man that communicates often, is so deified, that he seems to be a little god upon earth. And to such as he it is said: "You are gods, and the sons of the highest."‡ Go now, and bury these little gods in Purgatory: you will sooner work a miracle, and turn Purgatory into Paradise: for certainly Purgatory cannot be a fit place for those that are gods by participation, or consorts of the Divine nature, as St. Peter § terms them. If the sheep's teeth, that feed upon a certain herb in Candia, seem to be made of pure gold, what must we think of those, that are daily nourished with this Divine plant of Paradise, *Lilium convallium*, but that they have hearts of gold, consciences of gold, and so pure and refined gold, that the fire of Purgatory can find nothing more to purify and refine in them?

§ 12.—*The twelfth, a Faithful and Exact Obedience.*

The twelfth and last means to prevent Purgatory, which I intend here to propose, is an exact and faithful obedience; for I cannot persuade myself that

---

* Ambros. *Opusc. de Sanct. Sacram.*   † Cyp. *De Cœna Dom.*
‡ Psalm lxxxi. 6.   § 2 St. Peter i. 4.

a true obedient person will have much cause to fear
Purgatory.

Elias flew up to heaven in a fiery chariot; how
could he do it without burning? very well; for he did
it to obey God. The three children went into the
Babylonian furnace; alas! they are lost creatures.
No: for they went in to obey God. This being so,
be of good comfort: the fire knows not how to arm
itself against obedience. Jonas lies three days floating in a whale's belly: sure he is undone: the poor
man will never appear more. He will, he will; and
quickly too: for though it was his disobedience which
made him a prey to that devouring monster of the
sea, yet he now willingly submits to the decrees of
heaven; and, were it to do again, would as willingly
cast himself in, to obey the will of God; and since it
is so, he will infallibly recover his liberty, and not lose
the least hair of his head.

Moses walks in the bottom of the Red Sea, while
the waters stand like mountains on both sides, threat-
ening death and destruction. Alas! it were great pity
so worthy a person should be thus lost in waves.
Fear not; there is no danger. No; since he entered
to obey God, neither the sea, nor death, dare attempt
anything against him: all the elements have too much
respect to his obedience, to do him the least injury.
Daniel is in the lion's jaws: who put him there?
Obedience. Fear nothing; he will not perish: the
cruel lions will be his lifeguard, to protect him.
Behold Susanna, under a cloud of stones ready to
hail down upon her; who put her there? Obedience
to the law of God. And therefore do not fear; she

will come off untouched. All creatures do so highly
honour the commands of their Creator, that they will
sooner forget their own nature than forget to obey
Him, and honour all those who had rather die
than disobey. It is a kind of martyrdom, says
St. Thomas, to die for obedience; and, without
question, Purgatory was not made for martyrs. It is
a perfect holocaust, to sacrifice his life upon the altar
of obedience; and why should a heart, thus burnt and
consumed in obeying, be any more exposed to fire?
St. Bernard, in his funeral sermon of Humbertus, says,
that if that holy monk had anything to suffer in Purgatory, it was for want of a little obedience, in that
which concerned the care of his health; and that,
otherwise, he could not but think that he went immediately into heaven. Let us hear the great St. Ambrose.*
Whosoever, says he, does the will of God, who lived
and died in obedience, shall not die eternally; but at
the hour of his death shall hear those comfortable
words which were spoken to the good thief: "This
day thou shalt be with Me in Paradise." Why so? Is
it not sufficient that St. Ambrose speaks it so roundly?
But, if you will have a pertinent reason for it, take
this. The Angelical Doctor,† having first laid down
this position, that all eminent and heroical virtues
put a soul into a most pure and perfect state, says
further, a man can give God nothing that is of more
value in this miserable life, than to consecrate his will,
and submit it not only to Him, but, for love of Him,
to frail creatures, perhaps ignorant, hasty, and choleric,
perhaps younger, and less understanding than himself,

* In Psalm 39.   † 2. 2. q. 186. a. 5.

perhaps his own scholar, his own son, and, if you will, haply his own servant. Is not this a sublime kind of martyrdom, which ends not in a moment, or with one dint of a sword; but must endure a thousand strokes of an indiscreet tongue, which go more to the quick, and this all the days of his life? Now, is there any reason why a man that has courageously suffered all these martyrdoms, should be martyred again in Purgatory fire?

When Abraham, out of pure obedience, would have sacrificed his dear Isaac, God seemed so well pleased (I had almost said obliged to him for it,) that by way of requital, He made a solemn oath, to give him His only Son, and the land of promise, flowing with all manner of delights. Tell me; is not every obedient person another Abraham? nay, is he not greater than Abraham? since it is a far harder task for a man to sacrifice himself, then to sacrifice his son; to sacrifice, I say, his will, the noblest part of man, which is born to be sole empress of the universe, and has no other life but to rule and command, as well in the great as the lesser world? Now, let him be but another Abraham; and sure you will not think it fit to send him to Purgatory, who carries in his bosom the delights of Paradise? The Abbot Mutius, when he turned monk, brought his only son with him to the monastery, about eight years old, that he might begin betimes to learn the fear of God. The abbot of the monastery, to make trial of his obedience, peremptorily commands him to take the child, and throw him into the river: for he did nothing but disquiet the monks. The holy man, without disputing the case, animated with an angelical obedience, and a heart like that of Abraham, takes up the child, runs away with him to the river, throws him in, and returns again with dry eyes, and without any sign of trouble; as if he were not at all concerned for the loss of his own child. And certainly the child had been drowned, had not certain monks, who could swim well, lain secretly there, by the abbot's appointment; who took up this little Moses, saved this Isaac, and brought him back to the monastery, where they all stood in admiration of so perfect an example of blind obedience and self-denial, in so natural and lawful an affection, as is the love of a parent to his dear child.* The same day it was revealed to the abbot, that this act of Mutius was as pleasing to God as that of Abraham; and that he should be eternally blessed for it. Go, now, and cast this soul into Purgatory, who stuck not to cast his only son, I mean his obedience, into the river, at the command of his Superior; and when you have done this, will they not sooner, think you, cast in the whole river, which was thus blessed by a perfect act of obedience, and so quench the flames, than suffer her to lie burning there? Mutius did but once cast his son into the river; and how many religious souls, out of the same spirit of obedience, expose themselves a thousand times, to all dangers both by sea and land: and, after all this, must they needs visit Purgatory in their way to heaven?

It seems boldly said by St. Austin,† that the Blessed Virgin was happier in obeying God than in being the

* Cass. l. 4, c. 27.
† Tract. 10 in Joan.

Mother of God : and yet Christ Himself said as much
in express terms.

For when, by way of applauding Him,* they were
crying up her as blessed and happy, that had the
honour to be His Mother, and to nourish Him with
the milk of her breasts, He at once replied, that He
accounted them to be happy indeed, that heard His
word, and put it in practice. And, another time,†
when they had told Him that His good Mother, and
His brothers, stood without, waiting for Him; "Who,"
said He, " are My brothers, and whom do you call
My Mother? Whosoever does the will of My Father,
he is My mother, My brothers, and My whole parent-
age." Now, to our purpose ; if an obedient person
have the honour to bear this honourable title, of being
the brother, and even the mother, of God, can God so
far neglect this brother and mother of His, as to leave
them in Purgatory fire?

The abbess one day commanded St. Catharine of
Bologna,‡ that for the love of God, and the exercise
of obedience, she would enter into a burning furnace.
The Saint runs away instantly, and doubtless would
have thrown herself in ; had not the religious stood
in the way to hinder her. It is not a crime, says
St. Austin,§ to be thus prodigal of our lives, and even,
like Samson, to make ourselves away, when God
requires it. No ; this is no crime, but a pious holo-
canst, offered upon the altar of obedience : and will
you then kill a man that is already dead? will you
burn him in Purgatory, that is already consumed in

* St. Luke xi. 27, 28.   † St. Luke viii. 21.
‡ Lib. i. vitæ ejus.   § De Civ. c. i.

the holy flames of obedience? God does not use to punish, or purge, the same fault twice; and therefore a soul that has been once purged in the fire of obedience, hath no need of being purged again in the fire of Purgatory.

Oh, what a thing it is to be obedient! cried Gerard, as he lay a-dying in St. Bernard's arms. I have been carried before God's high tribunal, and have seen the power of obedience: nobody shall ever perish that is truly obedient; but, when he comes to die, shall mount above the choirs of Angels, Archangels, and Apostles, according to the merit of his obedience! and, with this, he died. Must Angels, Archangels, Apostles, and those that are in the same degree of perfection, be thrust into Purgatory fire? Is it reasonable, that they should be confined to so loathsome a prison, that made themselves voluntary prisoners under the severe government of obedience? I am resolved, said holy David, to fear no evils,* of what rugged nature soever they be, so long as Thou, my God, dost lead me by the hand. Though I should walk in the midst of the shadow of death, in the very suburbs of hell, which is Purgatory, I will fear nothing; for Thy rod, and Thy staff, wherewith Thou dost govern and direct me to do Thy holy will in all occasions, will be my sure comfort and protection.

An obedient man speaks nothing but victories, says the Holy Ghost, in the Proverbs.† What victories? Such as St. Dorotheus describes,‡ when he tells us, that a soul being seated in her triumphant chariot, drawn by humility and obedience, treads all under

* Psalm xxii. 4. † Prov. xxi. 28. ‡ Doct. i.

foot, and with a swift motion steers her course up to heaven. If humility and obedience be her horses, they will not easily convey her into Purgatory; for they know not the way thither, but only into heaven, their own native country: where they will be sure to leave this triumphant and victorious soul in the joyful fruition of eternal happiness. Take away self-will, and there will be no hell, cries St. Bernard.* If obedience can put out hell-fire, she must needs have power to put out the fire of Purgatory. What a solid comfort must this be to religious souls, who have given themselves over to the practice of this virtue: and to all those that, living in the world, yet do nothing of their own heads, but are constantly ruled by the will of God?

It is a strange but very true observation of St. Gregory, and of St. Bonaventure,† that God, who is invincible, will yet suffer Himself to be overcome by the obedience of His servants, so far as even to obey them: I say, obey; for it is the very expression He uses Himself in the case of Josue, who is said to have stopped the sun in his full career, because God was pleased to obey the voice of His obedient servant. If this be so, that God will refuse nothing to an obedient soul! let her ask Him to be freed from Purgatory; and she will not be denied it, who never denied Him anything. And without all doubt, it is as easy for her to curb the fire of Purgatory, as to stop the swift motion of the heavens. You, then, that are obedient, know your power; you

---

* *Serm.* I. *De Resurr.*
† Bonav. *Reg. Novit.* tom. vii. c. 13.

may appeal from God to God, in case He should sentence you to Purgatory; you may boldly claim His promise of denying you nothing; and then you will be sure to insert it in your bargain, to have nothing to do with Purgatory, but to go straight into heaven, there to enjoy Him for ever.

The Conclusion.

It is now high time to conclude this section, and, with it, the whole treatise. And I cannot leave you better than in heaven, whither I have brought you, if you will it yourself; for you see, it is in your power to make your way thither, without passing through Purgatory. Believe me, it is no trifling matter, but the most important business we have to do in this world, to purchase heaven; and to purchase it so, as to have right to take possession of it, immediately after we have left this world. Christ our Saviour tells us, that the kingdom of heaven suffers violence, and that they must be both violent and valiant that run away with it. Whereon St. Ambrose* observes well, that God loves to be forced; and that they who importune Him most, and use the greatest violence, are the men He makes most of. Take courage, then, dear reader; take courage! Imitate the good thief; snatch heaven out of His hands; steal away His Paradise; do something worthy of Him, worthy of yourself, and worthy of Paradise. If no better means occur to you, at least strive to be hugely concerned for the poor souls in Purgatory·

* St. Ambrose in *Luc.*

P

pray often and devoutly for them, and procure that good store of Masses may be said for their relief. You have the ell in your hands, by which you may measure out your own happiness; says the devout Salvian: be charitable to others, and they will be no less to you. The time is not long that is allowed you to sojourn in this world: in this little time, be sure you make the Saints in heaven, and the souls in Purgatory, your friends; that they be obliged to help you in your greatest need. Learn, at least, by these discourses, to have a tender heart for the poor souls, and to use your uttermost endeavour to go yourself directly into heaven out of this wicked world. It is the thing I earnestly beg of God's infinite mercy for you, and for myself, at the instance of your good prayers. For though I must acknowledge, I have deserved nothing but hell-fire, and have reason to take it for a high favour to be sent into Purgatory, to lie there as many months and years as it shall please God; yet I confess ingenuously, I have no great mind to either place, but only to heaven; which I beseech God, by the merits of my dear Saviour, and by the Plenary Indulgence of His most infinite mercy, to grant us all. Amen.

Et fidelium animæ per misericordiam Dei
requiescant in pace. Amen.

ERRATA.

Page 3, line 7, for *strage* read *strange.*
Page 11, line 16, for *holy water* read *holy water?*
Page 72, line 21, for *perfer* read *prefer.*
Page 195, line 21, for *all his : life* read *all his life :*

ST. JOSEPH'S ASCETICAL LIBRARY.

Edited by Fathers of the Society of Jesus.

LONDON : BURNS & OATES, 17 PORTMAN STREET.

Lightning Source UK Ltd.
Milton Keynes UK
UKOW06f2037061016

284668UK00016B/429/P